THE ELEGANT SOLUTION

Toyota's Formula for Mastering Innovation

MATTHEW E. MAY

Foreword by Kevin Roberts,
CEO Worldwide, Saatchi & Saatchi

FREE PRESS

New York   London   Toronto   Sydney

*f*P

FREE PRESS
A Division of Simon & Schuster, Inc.
1230 Avenue of the Americas
New York, NY 10020

FREE PRESS and colophon are trademarks of Simon & Schuster, Inc.

For infomation about special discounts for bulk purchases,
please contact Simon & Schuster Special Sales:
1-800-456-6798 or business@simonandschuster.com.

Designed by Matthew E. May

Manufactured in the United States of America

10   9   8   7   6   5   4   3   2   1

Library of Congress Cataloging-in-Publication Data
May, Matthew E.
The elegant solution: Toyota's formula for mastering innovation / Matthew E. May;
foreword by Kevin Roberts.
p. cm.
Includes bibliographical references and index.
1. Toyota Jido'sha Kabushi Kaisha. 2. Automobile industry and
trade—Management—Employee participation—Japan. 3. Automobile industry
and trade—Technological innovations—Japan. 4. Creative thinking. I. Title.
HD9710 .J34 T63655   2006
658.4'063—dc22   2006048411

ISBN-13: 978-0-7432-9017-3
ISBN-10:   0-7432-9017-8

There's a way to do it better—find it.
Thomas Edison

CONTENTS

Foreword

The world loves Toyota. This book goes a long way in explaining why.

As their competitors all over the world struggle with being industrial organizations in a postindustrial world, Toyota moves forward. On any measure—customer loyalty, vehicle quality, profit, output volume, best-selling new models, innovation, sustainability—Toyota is magnificent.

How does Toyota do it?

Many have attempted an explanation, but none can match this one. Matthew May's collected learnings are those of an insider, someone who has stood shoulder to shoulder with his teammates on the line of scrimmage playing for Toyota. An educator on innovation at Toyota's university, Matthew has seen up close the big structures and systems, as well as the details, the smallest things in the day-to-day running of the world's best car company.

If there is such a thing as the quintessential postindustrial organization, then perhaps its picture is painted in this book. It's the picture of a highly structured and systematized culture that is also a hotbed of individual creativity. For Toyota, innovation is the mastery of "thinking *within* the box." This duality—systems and creativity—must be close to the essence of Toyota's organizational genius. The system gives the individual worker purpose, direction, and a sense of belonging. It creates a momentum that becomes self-generative.

This book tells a story of Toyota as a living entity, always seeking to "find and fit the rhythm of the change happening around it." An organization created more than one hundred years ago and looking stronger with each year that passes, Toyota has discovered the secret of evolution.

The secret is the interplay between a system strong enough and bold enough to inspire loyalty beyond reason and the creative performers within that system. And where is that system firmly focused? On customers. And on the environment.

For me, the key passage in this book is the inspiring story of Paul Guitierrez, the autoworker from the GM plant in Fremont, California, that Toyota turned around in the 1980s. Before Toyota, Fremont was a soul-destroying hole that turned out appallingly made cars. Toyota arrived, introduced the workers to its system, and then invited them to perfect it. Suddenly the workers were proud of their work and talking about being creative every day on the job. Creativity on an assembly line? The idea seemed oxymoronic.

Then, in a single year, the new organization instigated more than eight thousand performance improvement ideas from people on the line. This story of Toyota is a modern business parable: Greatness comes to the biggest when they harness the spirit of the many.

—Kevin Roberts

Kevin Roberts is CEO Worldwide of the ideas company Saatchi & Saatchi, the principal global advertising partner of Toyota (since 1972) and Lexus. He is also CEO in Residence at Cambridge University's Judge Institute of Management and Professor of Sustainable Enterprise at both the University of Waikato Management School in New Zealand and the University of Limerick in Ireland. He is the author of three books: Lovemarks: The Future Beyond Brands *(powerHouse Books, 2004),* SiSoMo: The Future on Screen *(powerHouse Books, 2005), and* The Lovemarks Effect: Winning in the Consumer Revolution *(powerHouse Books, 2006). He is co-author of* Peak Performance: Business Lessons from the World's Top Sports Organizations *(Texere, 2002).*

One Million Ideas

The best way to get a good idea is to get a lot of ideas.
Linus Pauling

Who needs another book on innovation?

The world. But it better be different. It better look at innovation through a new lens. And it better be something that helps with the daily work, because the innovation that's long been the badge of American business is slowly being siphoned off. Outsourced. And that's bad news. Nothing creates customer value like innovation. Innovation is a core company process. It's not a department, it's everyone's responsibility. Export it, and with it goes a significant chunk of valuable contribution and competitive advantage.

There's a ray of hope. The Toyota organization implements a million ideas a year. It's fact.

One million.

Ponder that number for a minute. For most people, that figure conjures up visions of winning the lottery, or a dream home, or a superstar salary, or the number of people on the road during rush hour.

One million seems like an impossible target if you're talking about business ideas. But it's not, at least not for Toyota. It's the real reason why their nearly $150 billion-plus market value outstrips GM, Ford, Daimler-Chrysler, Honda, and Volkswagen put together. It's the reason they're one of the planet's ten most profitable companies. It's why they make well over twice as much money as any other carmaker, and with under 15% of the market. It's why their systems, processes, and products are the envy of the world. It's the greatest source of their competitive advantage and staying power. It's their engine of innovation.

Those ideas are coming from every level in the organization. Because innovation isn't about technology. And it's certainly not about manufacturing. It's about value, and opportunity, and impact. At Toyota, *every idea counts*. It's an environment of everyday innovation, the direct result of a fanatical focus on getting a little better, daily.

Good enough never is. When your whole company thinks like that, you're unstoppable.

The business world is taking notice. Organizations from all over the world are knocking on Toyota's doors to learn the basis of their uncanny ability to consistently achieve breakthroughs, big and small. They're seeking the Holy Grail of operational optimization, because they know that innovation is taking on a new shape. They know that the next wave of innovative energy won't be narrowly focused on product and service quality, because we're closing in on parity and commoditization across the board. They know that what's next is all about thinking differently, about how to create compelling customer value, about how to flow that value through streamlined processes, and about embedding a real discipline around the pursuit of perfection. They're finding that they too can tap into the kind of thinking that has led Toyota to be one of the truly great success stories in business.

> If you are not busy reinventing your company, I guarantee you are falling backwards.
> **Fujio Cho**
> Vice Chairman, Toyota

And that's where *The Elegant Solution* fits in. It all started with a ridiculous assignment: *"We need to translate the Toyota Production System for the knowledge worker. We really want to figure out how to bring the levels of employee productivity, engagement, continuous improvement and constant creativity found in our Toyota factories and warehouses to the corporate environment."*

Huh? It didn't make any sense. Everyone knows factory work isn't creative, right? But that was my charge in 1999, commissioned by a new client, the then-dean of the newly formed University of Toyota, a "Toyota New Era" strategic initiative funded by Toyota's U.S. marketing arm,

Toyota Motor Sales, U.S.A., Inc. Shouldn't it be the other way around, I thought—helping assembly line workers and parts pickers to find the kind of satisfaction and success skilled professionals enjoy?

So I stalked the production environment for months, guided by a master of everyday innovation. I got trained in the Toyota Production System. I learned how the principles applied to parts supply chain management and logistics. I learned how to prepare a one-page report—called an A3, in reference to its paper size—capturing the story of how a specific problem is solved. And I did what any normal investigator would do: study the processes, gather information, talk to people, lift the visible techniques, and try to fabricate some conceptual model to make sense out of the findings and show how smart I was.

The problem was, I seemed to be getting dumber every day. I soon found out how little I knew about real-world problem solving and business creativity. Each day, my assignment got harder. The workers *were* more engaged and creative than their corporate counterparts. The jobs weren't creative, the job was to *be* creative, daily. I did my best to try and absorb it all. I realized there was no way to quickly understand and internalize this stuff. I'd have to live it and breathe it for a while first. I would have to work from the inside out, not the other way around.

So I did. I became so deeply involved with Toyota that they bought all my time for several years. No longer was I the observer, but an extended team member. I learned from the best, and participated fully. Over the course of several years, I moved from novice to journeyman to expert. I got to design and deliver the key homegrown University of Toyota programs. I built original education now used by Toyota associates all over the world to grasp The Toyota Way. It took over a half decade, through all manner of fits and starts, but not only did the original translation project eventually morph into a tremendously successful internal program, but the University of Toyota began selectively offering it to other organizations, like Wells Fargo, Sprint Nextel, Gallup, Quadrant Homes, Department of Defense, and the Los Angeles Police Department.

Toyota sent *me* to work with those organizations.

That's what makes this book so very different from any other. There's something universally applicable here. That's hard to come by. There are already plenty of books on Toyota's vaunted production system. I'm far more interested in the human-centered creative process behind what is really just the visible result of a much deeper dynamic. For, you see, the Toyota Production System is an elegant solution, the manifest outcome of an invisible discipline around innovative problem solving.

And there are plenty of books by people who study innovation from high altitudes. As a rule, the grand strategies just don't travel well. They're not actionable, so you won't find any here. Just what I *know* from firsthand experience to be the driving forces behind the kinds of outcomes Toyota and their brethren enjoy. What's missing is a winning formula for how to cultivate ideas at every level in the company and convert them to value for customers.

> *Bold ideas, careful action.*
> **Kiichiro Toyoda**

I've worked with managers to turn ideas into action for over twenty years, and in as many different organizations. Toyota is a breed apart. No other company so correctly and consistently does all the right things right, and so well. If I've learned anything in my time with Toyota, I've learned to seek the *elegant solution*—the singular and deceptively simple idea with huge impact that lies beyond the enormous complexity of the challenging business problems we all face in our companies. What's most compelling is that it doesn't matter whether you're talking about the design of the new Scion, the engineering of advanced hybrid technology, the little improvements made daily on the shop floor, or the process enhancements in the back office operations—the central precepts and creative processes for mastering innovation are the same. Opportunity for impact is always relative to one's level of responsibility, but the core process is the same.

Thus the basic proposition: *The quest for the elegant solution shapes true innovation.*

It's worked for Toyota for over a century. It's worked for others, and it can work for you.

The formula for the elegant solution is an amalgam of principles, practices, and protocol. Part 1 is all about the deeper principles. Principles drive practices. They're so important that each one deserves its own chapter. Principles aren't enough, though. You have to make them operational with ten key practices supported by tools and techniques. You may or may not need them all. You can choose what works for you, your team, your organization. That's Part 2. But just having a toolbox and knowing how to use the tools doesn't necessarily make you a master craftsman. You still have to build something. You have to know how to put the practices and tools together well to achieve a result. You'll track the course of a team through a day of searching for the elegant solution, using all ten practices. And that's Part 3.

> *Keep in mind what I call the three C's for innovation. The first C is for creativity. The second C is for challenge. The third C is for courage.*
> **Shoichiro Toyoda**

I should tell you up front that none of the individual concepts are new, or even unique to Toyota. The dozens of non-Toyota cases included should bear that out. Rather, the magic is found in Toyota's remarkable ability to collectively and completely master all of them *as a way of life*, not a program centered on select teams led by specialists with artificial agendas. *That's* what makes Toyota unique, and worth studying.

In *The Elegant Solution,* I'll share with you what I've learned. And show you how it's all done, hopefully in a way you find elegant and innovative. If I've done my job right, you should have a pretty good road map for conducting your own search for elegant solutions.

—Matthew May

In Search of Elegance

I would not give a fig for the simplicity this side of complexity, but I would give my life for the simplicity on the other side of complexity.
Oliver Wendell Holmes

It's Not About the Gizmo

Scene:

Kosai, Shizuoka Prefecture, Japan. Circa 1888. Japan has opened its doors to the world—two decades into the Meiji Reformation, two years into the Japan Patent Law.

A young man watches his mother slave all day in the rafters of their humble home to weave clothing on a manual spinning loom, a primitive tool unchanged for centuries. It pains him to see her scrap a hard day's work because of a single broken thread in the finished garment. Barely 20, inventive, energetic, and eager to change the world—carpentry is his trade, but not his calling. Ignoring elder disapproval, he challenges himself to build a better loom, sketching prototypes, building test models, and applying his woodworking skills in creative ways that others view as eccentric. He receives a patent for a handloom that improves quality and productivity dramatically. He's not satisfied. He turns his attention to developing a power loom.

By 1898, he perfects Japan's first steam-powered loom, which allows textile mills to quadruple productivity and halve costs. His looms are the highest quality, lowest cost, and easiest to use—putting the finest German and French looms to shame. Business booms, and his star rises quickly in Japan. His quest to perfect drives him ever forward, creating a

In those days, spinning and weaving was not a thriving business as it is today. The work was done by old women sitting at home and weaving the cloth by hand. Although everybody in my village was a farmer, every house also had its own handloom. I began thinking about ways to power the looms so that weaving could be done faster, and more cloth could be made more cheaply. People could then buy cotton goods for less, and that would benefit society substantially.

Sakichi Toyoda

string of tiny innovations in rapid succession. Three decades into his search, he designs a mechanism to automatically halt the loom whenever a thread breaks. It changes the world. It takes five more years to perfect. And so from small but steady improvements with radical results and a strong desire to help people is born Toyoda Automatic Loom Works, the precursor to Toyota Motor Company.

Nearly a lifetime in the offing, Sakichi Toyoda finds the elegant solution.

The story of Sakichi Toyoda is not about invention, or about the technological development of the automatic loom in Japan. It's about one man's nearly spiritual quest to solve a very real problem facing the world around him.

If you read closely, three underlying principles come into clear view:

- *Ingenuity in craft*
- *Pursuit of perfection*
- *Fit with society*

These are the very principles that to this day fuel the engine of innovation at Toyota. They form the basis for everything Toyota does. In fact, they are the deeper principles behind nearly every great innovation the world has ever seen.

But how easily we forget! Mention innovation, and people immediately think, *technology*.

The truth is that business innovation is about satisfaction and value, not new gadgetry. The pace of technological progress sweeps us off our feet and we get all caught up in the gizmo, losing sight of the *why* behind the *what*. Customers don't want products and services, they want solutions to problems. Nobody raised a hand to ask for an automatic loom. Perhaps that's why looms hadn't changed much over the years until Sakichi came on the scene.

> *Above all, innovation is not invention. It is a term of economics rather than of technology.*
> **Peter Drucker**

And when it comes to solutions, simple is better. Elegant is better still. Elegance is the simplicity found on the far side of complexity.

Elegance Afield

The rice fields of Y2K Laos are an unlikely birthplace for an elegant solution to a problem that industry's largest companies still struggle to solve. The country is destitute, almost primitive. Remains of the Vietnam War litter the landscape. Bicycle is the chief mode of transportation. Few homes have everyday conveniences of electricity and telephones, much less computers and access to the Internet. Rice is an economic mainstay, and the basis for one of few viable markets. Almost everyone grows rice. Yet farmers remain ignorant of the price of rice in the adjacent village, for the information simply isn't available. Until...

A young man with knowledge of telecom infrastructure sets about the task of keeping rice farmers informed. In a world far behind and unconnected, he creates a universal wireless email system by connecting old computers through cheap antennas. Cost for the rig? Less than $200. He is undaunted by the lack of electricity, powering his system with the one resource readily available: human pedal power. It is a two-man operation with a simple schematic. One person pedals a stationary bike wired to a small generator that produces the electricity needed to boot the computer, and the other sends the email message containing the current price of rice. The system rapidly spreads to network status, covering all of Laos and connecting it to the Internet through the only site with access, the capital city of Vientiane.

While elsewhere world governments and big business fight over the wireless spectrum to create and profit from third generation (3G) wireless networks, Laos deploys a simple universal wireless system for those in need of a real-time price quote on rice to compete with neighboring villages.

It's not pretty, modern, or sophisticated. But it's elegant.

DEFINING ELEGANCE

Great innovation is nearly impossible without understanding and appreciating the concept of elegance as it relates to solving important problems.

Elegance isn't about being hoity-toity. It's not about lofty concepts and grand designs. It's not about beauty or grace, or anything to do with aesthetics—ugly is okay. Elegance is about something much more profound. It's about finding the *aha* solution to a problem with the greatest parsimony of effort and expense. Creativity plays a part. Simplicity plays a part. Intelligence plays a part. Add in subtlety, economy, and quality, and you get elegance.

The effects of elegant solutions are significant, ranging from understated intellectual appreciation to truly seismic change. Elegant solutions relieve creative tension by solving the problem *in finito* as it's been defined, in a way that avoids creating other problems that then need to be solved. Elegant solutions render only new possibilities to chase and exploit.

Finally, elegant solutions aren't obvious, except, of course, in retrospect.

DEFINING INNOVATION

A lot has been written about innovation. How it's distinct from creativity. How it goes beyond improvement. How it entails seeking and taking big risks. How it's all about big ideas and radical departures from convention. How it means completely scrapping the old system. How it's limited to the right-brainers, and suits need not apply. How you need deep pockets just to play the game.

Those biases are limiting at best, and only

The Elegant Solution

An elegant solution is one in which the optimal or desired effect is achieved with the least amount of effort.

Engineers seek the elegant solution as a means of solving a problem with the least possible waste of resources. In a mathematical proof, elegance is the minimum number of steps to achieve the solution with greatest clarity. In dance or the martial arts, elegance is minimum motion with maximum effect. In filmmaking, elegance is a simple message with complex meaning.

An elegant solution is recognized by its juxtaposition of simplicity and power. The most challenging games have the fewest rules, as do the most dynamic societies and organizations.

An elegant solution is quite often a single tiny idea that changes everything.

Toyota and Elegant Solutions: Strange Bedfellows?

Elegant solutions embrace an overarching philosophy of doing far more with much less, a notion that has become synonymous with Toyota and is present to this day in all of their operations, from design and engineering to manufacturing and distribution to sales and marketing. Production seeks to drive out waste to become leaner. Engineering seeks a certain simplicity in product design. Research seeks greater fuel economy through hybrid energy.

Which begs the question: How did it become such a central part of the organizational genetics?

Answer: Necessity.

World War II left industrial Japan in tatters, including Toyota Motor, which was started in the late 1930s by Kiichiro Toyoda, son of Sakichi Toyoda. The need to survive and thrive amid a scarcity of business essentials—land, facilities, money, and labor—mandated a new way of thinking and conducting business. Intent on competing successfully in the world automotive market but lacking the luxury of abundant resources, Toyota did the only thing they could do: search for ways to accomplish more with less.

How? Leverage what they *did* have: deeply-rooted values of employee ingenuity, constant improvement, and a strong will to serve society.

serve to exclude the everyman from innovating. The best definition of innovation on the planet is the one given by David Neeleman, founder and CEO of JetBlue: *"Innovation is trying to figure out a way to do something better than it's ever been done before."* Thomas Edison would agree.

The definition is an elegant solution in itself, because it wrestles to the ground a complex, hotly contested concept and makes it accessible to everyone, at every level. It renders irrelevant all the silly distinctions between different theoretical classes of innovation—with a single stroke, the conceptual difference between constant improvement and break-through innovation becomes useless. It removes the prevailing mystique, and begs no further explanation. And it would be wrong to think it doesn't include things that have never been done before. Because everything has a precursor at some level, somewhere. It's just that it hasn't quite been pinpointed correctly.

So from here on, when we refer to innovation, we mean solving the problem of how to do something better than ever.

The Temptations

Elegant solutions are all around us, waiting to be discovered. But they're no easy challenge. Elegant solutions require a working knowledge of the forces at play, and obstacles in the way. Aside from what is invariably mislabeled and sloppily defined as *culture*—and more on that later—a few big traps can stop elegant innovation cold. They are three in number, easy to fall into, and most appropriately termed *temptations:*

1. Swinging for fences. This is the "home run or bust" trap, which invariably destroys a strong batting average over time. It carries with it huge risk, usually accompanied by high cost.

2. Getting too clever. This is the "bells and whistles" trap, which can easily get out of control in an effort to outdo competitors. It carries with it the danger of complexity and customer alienation.

Elegant Solutions

Many of the most powerful innovations are singular and deceptively simple ideas that universally change the world's attitudes, beliefs, behaviors, and habits. Examples:
• Library
• Paper money
• Pencil
• Wallet
• Wristwatch
• Icebox
• Mortgage
• Social Security
• Credit card
• Cell phone
• Auto leasing

3. Solving problems frivolously. This is the "brainstorm" trap, which is misguided creativity far afield from company direction. It's a symptom of poorly defined work, and fraught with waste.

History has shown that sustainable business innovation isn't as much about throwing the Hail Mary pass as about running a solid ground game. Companies that have truly mastered innovation know that it can be "derisked" by making a number of small bets across a portfolio of ideas, rather than one big bet-the-farm gamble on a would-be killer app. To win consistently over the long haul takes strong disciplines and solid routines for solving problems and chasing opportunities.

But how do you know if you're heading in the right direction? One answer is to start with the little stuff that helps in the daily work, like Sakichi Toyoda did. Adopt his three principles, take them as your own, and make them yours. Because principles go a long way toward overcoming the temptations by offering the necessary guidance to the problem-solving effort.

Poetry in Motion

Cyclist Lance Armstrong discovered that he could climb a mountain better by standing and spinning lower gears at a much higher cadence than the widely accepted practice of driving big gears while seated. He took a scientific approach to a problem; namely, *what's the best way to climb a mountain on a bike, given my gifts?* By accepting and respecting the limitation of the medium, he leveraged the constraints in his effort to drive new ideas and methods.

His record may never be matched: seven consecutive Tour de France titles.

THE ART OF INGENUITY

The pressure to innovate in a fiercely competitive marketplace falls on the individual: we're asked for higher commitment, more adaptability, quicker progress, better execution, stronger decision making, and freer thinking. At the same time, we're told to manage risk, meet short-term objectives, and only bet on sure things. All within the confines of environments that are often anything but free: powerful systems, rigid structures, conflicting agendas, privileged information, political posturing, and limiting rules.

The truth is that uncertainty, risk, and failure are all part of innovation, and the ability to meet business objectives doesn't always square with the personal capabilities needed to innovate as required. Solution: Work like an artist. Work like a scientist.

How? By exploiting your expertise; by pursuing possibility; courageously rejecting the status quo; viewing opposition as an inventive challenge; refusing to let bureaucracy and hierarchy stifle your creativity; using cutbacks and resource constraints to drive new ideas and methods. By pursuing the simple question that drives the kind of "new-school" thinking found at the heart of every breakthrough, big or small: *Is there a better way?*

THE PURSUIT OF PERFECTION

Let's drop the conventional distinction between "incremental" and "breakthrough" innovation. Perhaps valuable in theory, it simply isn't useful in any practical way.

While a handful of game-changing innovations can be traced to a stroke of genius, the vast majority of effective innovations in industry result from a rigorous search for the optimal solution. Furthermore, unexpected thunderbolt breakthroughs have little place in the strategic scheme of things, because they're very often one-offs or happy accidents, and not repeatable. You can't build a business on serendipity. It's romantic, but it's not predictable or reliable.

The systematic pursuit of perfection *is*. It's the discipline of increments, and just plain hard work. Like it or not, the pursuit of perfection is everyone's job. It can't be departmentalized or outsourced. It's not limited to the Product Design or the R&D group. That kind of thinking only works to contain human creativity and squelch the spirit of innovation.

Chasing perfection transforms today into tomorrow by creating new processes, products, and services. The beauty of organized improvement lies in its ability to consistently yield low-cost, low-risk,

Racing Ahead
Toyota's Lexus brand is a modern-day version of *The Tortoise and the Hare.*
Toyota worked tirelessly at continuous improvement for forty-five years before launching the luxury line. It then took just two years to displace Mercedes-Benz and BMW, entrenched for generations, as the top-selling luxury import nameplate in America. Within 10 years, it was the leading luxury brand in the United States.
Lesson: Being first and fast in the short run isn't necessarily optimal in the long run.

high-impact breakthroughs. It prepares you to capitalize on the bigger opportunities when they come, so you won't miss out. Ultimately, the small steps catalyze something altogether new and novel. Innovation isn't an either-or proposition forcing a choice between small steps and big leaps.

It's how to achieve big leaps *through* small steps.

THE RHYTHM OF FIT

What distinguishes great innovation is its ability to serve the great needs of society with a valuable, meaningful contribution. Simply put, a successful mousetrap needs a serious rodent infestation, and a delivery system that places the mousetrap in the hands of those who can make the most use and best sense of it in today's terms.

And that requires a keen insight into the prevailing systems surrounding your business. You can fight for your marvelously bright idea, but chances are you'll lose in the long run to a competitor who figures out how to either leverage the current system to make the idea work with what's out there now, or offers a new system to deliver the idea. Either way, it takes *systems thinking*, defined as the ability to think well through cause and effect. And that entails understanding *context*. Because there's a certain rhythm to great innovation.

A great innovation *fits*—fits the innovator, fits the times, and fits within a larger system. A great innovation shapes the attitudes and behaviors of people. A great innovation, big or small, changes how people think and work. A great innovation allows others to see in it their own opportunity for a new and better life. A great innovation, like great leadership, aims to create change that matters.

Great innovation is elegant simplicity imbued with the power to move the world.

Don't Fight, Fit

While the rest of the music world fought the trend to share and download single songs over the Internet—defending to the death the old system under attack by music lovers—along comes Apple Computer, with a nifty little mp3 gizmo called the iPod. But not just another mp3 player. A whole system, iTunes, to deliver songs the way people were wanting them delivered, designed to allow the iPod and its user to fit seamlessly into the whole mechanism. Apple cut deals to make everyone gain. It adapted to the current reality.

It was *rhythmic*.

POINTS OF DEPARTURE

We face hundreds of problems and opportunities each day. We need some way to weed out the important ones, the right ones, the ones we should be working on—because those are the ones that demand elegant solutions.

The three principles of *ingenuity in craft, pursuit of perfection,* and *fit with society* guide the pathway to elegant solutions. Treated as policy, they lend the proper framework for the *practice* of innovation. They let us know if we're doing the right work. They inform our efforts by providing a solid focus, so actions and decisions become clearer. They put us in a better position to adapt to the rapidly changing landscape. They promote personal responsibility by requiring us to think through the immediate issues and summon our best judgment. Adhered to religiously, they prevent ideas for ideas' sake.

They're the *raison d'être* at Toyota, and nonnegotiable. But you'd be hard-pressed to locate any significant innovation *anywhere* or *by anyone* that can't be traced to some combination of these cornerstones.

So it's worth a closer look at each.

REFLECTION

What role does innovation play in your organization?

What guides the innovation efforts?

What was the focus of your most successful innovation?

What were the conditions of your last innovation?

How widespread is the spirit of innovation?

part 1

principles
light to work by

CHAPTER 1

The Art of Ingenuity

When I say artist I don't mean in the narrow sense of the word, but the man who is building things—creating, molding the earth. It's all a big game of construction—some with a brush, some with a shovel, some choose a pen.

Jackson Pollock

Everyman the Artist

Despite the alarm bells being sounded by the popular business press that innovation in America is in danger of becoming extinct, there's a slowly rising tide of creativity among today's workforce. More and more, people are beginning to return to the almost forgotten Renaissance era of mastery. They're adopting a different view of their work. In all walks of professional life, from senior executives to factory workers to part-timers, people are beginning to see themselves as artists and scientists, or more accurately, *business* artists and *business* scientists.

Why? First, because the current business environment demands it. In fact, it makes sense to say that the alleged outsourcing of innovation may just be at the root of it all. The demand for innovative thinking is at an all-time high and constantly increasing. *Someone's* getting the business. Competing for that business necessarily places personal ingenuity on par with business acumen as the needed professional capability.

Second, because this new millennium brings with it a general disenchantment with business, thanks in no small part to the fall from grace of once highly regarded executives, vaunted institutions, and respected professions. People need some way to think about their work, a new perspective that enables them to manage the mounting tension between their ability to innovate and the ever-increasing demands placed on them. They need a way to get a better sense of control over their work and life.

There's really no choice other than to take creative license. Management thinker Peter Drucker reminded us that business is about two things: marketing and innovation. Well, creativity is the essential element in both. Which means the slow evolution is likely to become a speedy revolution, one that will likely see business and creative skills converge to become the new work imperative. So much so that companies like Toyota, ServiceMaster, and Gore—all best in breed—are already there. Senior management of these companies sees innovation first and foremost as a matter of removing the typical organizational barriers to personal ingenuity and releasing the creative power of people.

> *Millions of Americans are beginning to work and live the way creative people like artists and scientists always have.*
> **Richard Florida,** Author
> *The Rise of the Creative Class*

The second question—*how?*—is far more interesting. And far more involved. The answer is best arrived at through a real story of personal ingenuity.

Thornton "Thor" Oxnard arrived in 1992 from the United States at Toyota's corporate headquarters in Nagoya, Japan with his MBA in one hand and MA in Japan Studies in the other, eager to put both to good use. He was promptly assigned to a month-long tour of duty in the factory, working on the assembly line. Immediately oriented to the ways of the Toyota Production System, he emerged with a basic knowledge of standardized work and lean manufacturing, and was transferred to the Overseas Parts Division. His assignment: Supply Analyst, processing overseas parts orders.

Feeling underutilized and somewhat disappointed, Thor performed his tasks as assigned, waiting patiently for his responsibilities to be increased. A month came and went without a change. "I know I'm capable of more," he thought. He approached his manager to request more work, and sat back to wait patiently to be told what to do. But the orders never came. Thor repeated his plea to no avail. Finally, on his third attempt, his manager explained: "We exposed you to the principles of Toyota Production System. We gave you a small starting assignment. You must determine the rest. You must tell me what needs to be done. You must dig your own job."

Thor was shocked. "I get to tell my manager what my job is?" This was the opposite of what he expected. Undaunted by the challenge posed by a lack of clear direction, Thor quickly became excited and engaged. "What an opportunity," he thought. "Create my own job!" He immediately embarked on his search for work.

Thor quickly realized that this would be no easy challenge. How would he figure out what needs to be done? Would it fit with his knowledge and skill? Would it add value to the organization? Would it be accepted by his manager?

He set about the task of talking to everyone he could. In the course of his exploration, he came to know the operation better. He came to see the bigger picture of how the various processes and departments worked together. He began to understand where his expertise might be best used.

Finally, Thor uncovered a problem. A contentious relationship existed between Toyota and General Motors with respect to the supply of parts to joint Toyota/GM operations in the United States. Upon further investigation, Thor found that the source of the contention was the lack of a supply contract. Why was there no contract? Thor kept digging. It seemed Toyota and GM couldn't agree to terms, so there was no basis for a contract. Why couldn't they agree? Why had the issue of operating without a contract suddenly become so important? Thor realized that the situation could present a real obstacle to Toyota's new parts distribution strategy.

> Observe...without preconceptions and with a blank mind. Repeat "why?" five times to every matter.
> **Taiichi Ohno**

Soon, he discovered that much of the disagreement centered on misunderstandings regarding Toyota policies, such as parts pricing. Why the misunderstanding? he wondered. Thor found by talking to others that, in general, Toyota had never really explained the rationale behind their policies regarding the supply of parts. For example, Toyota would not negotiate parts pricing, much to the consternation of GM. Why no negotiation? By talking to both parties using his bilingual skill, Thor quickly came to the conclusion that the root of the problem was to be found in the general lack of communication between Toyota and GM.

Communication was not occurring because neither party knew how to explain their position.

Thor had found his job: act as the liaison and interpreter to both parties and facilitate a contractual agreement. Thor immediately explained to GM that Toyota was bound to maintain price parity between what they supplied GM and what they supplied their Toyota-only operations. Therefore, Toyota would not, could not, negotiate. Further, GM didn't have to worry that prices would be raised indiscriminately: Toyota was bound by their U.S. operations to set reasonable, market-based prices. A contract was swiftly developed and agreed to by both parties.

Through the course of digging his own job, Thor Oxnard came to understand that the first principle of innovation—ingenuity in craft—was all about applied creativity.

Ten years later, Thor would play a pivotal role in one of Toyota's most ambitious supply-chain management initiatives, covered in a later chapter.

The story of Thor Oxnard reveals many of the key elements of personal ingenuity in the real world. It vividly captures the essence of what applied creativity in organizations actually looks like most of the time.

It's NOT sitting around dreaming up earth-shattering ideas behind closed doors, trying to be clever and creative in concocting a new secret sauce that will blow the doors off the competition. It *is* making best use of one's expertise while openly exploring possibility and defining the task at hand.

It's NOT a bevy of high-ranking executive managers involved in a costly and complex process engineered to boil the ocean. It *is* a frontline worker exploring, finding, and solving an important problem hands-on, down where the action is.

It's NOT an ivory tower edict with specific marching instructions handed down in a command-and-control fashion. It *is* a quick dip in the basic fundamentals followed by an open invitation to produce something of value, leaving open to individual interpretation how best to do so.

It's NOT about a company. It *is* about an individual—the right person with the right idea.

It's NOT about artistic expression. It *is* a compelling example of how the everyman can blend business skills with the mindset of the artist and discipline of the scientist.

And above all, Thor's story answers the question: *How do you start to invoke ingenuity in your craft?* It's really quite simple: ***Dig your own job!***

Sakichi Toyoda did it. Thor Oxnard did it. You can do it. Here's how.

CHASING INGENUITY

Ingenuity is equal parts creativity and application. And creativity as a concept scares the average corporate bloke, for two reasons.

First, because conventional wisdom treats it as a special quality, a mystical talent, selectively reserved for "le artiste" who waits for the kiss of the muse to inspire a masterpiece. Which is nonsense, but certainly convenient. By thinking of creativity as a natural gift, you can relieve accountability for ingenuity and excuse failure to innovate all in a single stroke. Second, because it seems somehow "soft" and unrelated to the hard-edged tactics thought to be needed to succeed on the business battlefield. It's okay for the advertising group, though.

> *Being good in business is the most fascinating kind of art. Making money is art and working is art and good business is the best art.*
> **Andy Warhol**

The reality of the situation is just the reverse. Every year, our work gets more complex. Business gets more competitive. Jobs get more specialized. Careers get less stable. Goals get more challenging. Budgets shrink. Deadlines tighten. And all the while, the pace of change just keeps accelerating. How are you going to deal with all that? You've got more to do and less to do it with. You have no choice other than to get more creative, more *resourceful*. That's the kind of applied creativity we're talking about. And there are two sides to the ingenuity coin:

Side A: Engagement

Side B: Exploration

Side A tells you *where* to dig. Side B tells you *how* to dig. Let's clarify the ideas.

Question

What does a Camry have in common with Gore-Tex?

Answer

They're both made by companies that push personal ingenuity and let associates dig their own job.

Toyota Motor Corporation, maker of the Camry, and W. L. Gore, the maker of Gore-Tex, both refer to employees as "associates." They both believe in job sculpting, allowing individuals to match talent to task. Gore goes one better, eliminating job titles entirely. In both companies, it may take months for someone to find their niche. And that's just the beginning—they then must establish their credibility by producing valuable, unique ideas.

And there's a bit more, as it turns out.

They both believe in the power of teams, and detest rigid hierarchy. At Toyota, the typical multilevel factory hierarchy and hundred-plus job descriptions have been replaced by a flattened team structure: team members and team leaders. Team members are cross-trained and may shift jobs as frequently as every two hours. At Gore, there are no bosses or supervisors or managers, only sponsors and mentors. The individual commitment is to the team.

Finally, both companies detest complacency, and worship constant forward movement. They both take a long view of innovation, favoring getting it *right* over getting it *out*.

No wonder both are best in class.

Side A: Engagement

Creativity depends largely on how you personally connect with your work. When the ties are strong, creativity flows more freely. When they're not, it's a real struggle.

You have to connect on two levels, *task* and *cause*. The first is about the *what* and the second is about the *why*.

Taskfit: The Rule of Four

Psychologists love to explain our uniquely hardwired capabilities in hugely complex terms. Sixteen types, thirty-four strengths, etc.

There's an easier, more elegant way of thinking about it. It all started about 2500 years ago, when Greek physician Hippocrates talked about the four "humours." Then philosopher Plato touted the four "faculties of the soul," followed by Aristotle, who focused on the four "sources of happiness." More modern thought follows suit: Erich Adickes spoke of four "worldviews." Eduard Spränger mentioned four "value attitudes." Carl Jung wrote of four "basic functions." Isabel Briggs Myers identified four "types." David Keirsey described four "temperaments." Most recently, The Gallup Organization's Strengths Theory splits its various strength themes into four main categories.

It's the *Rule of Four*. Take all of the work that's gone before, pare it back to something easier to grasp and more useful for the everyman, and you have the four basic buckets of natural ability:

- **Strategy**—you're an idea person, a *thoughtstarter*
- **Tactics**—you're an action person, a *playmaker*
- **Logistics**—you're a process person, a *taskmaster*
- **Diplomacy**—you're a people person, a *peacekeeper*

We all have some of each, but one defines our true sweet spot. That's where our greatest ingenuity comes from. That's the "dig zone."

Zoning In

You know it when you're "in the zone." You feel the flow. You feel independent, free to flex and stretch your abilities in pursuit of the goal, which always seems clear. Taking risks doesn't seem so scary, because the confidence is there. You define the work differently, expanding your role without giving it a second thought. You're far more resourceful than others. You use constraints as creative fuel, and see opportunities to improve and innovate that others don't. Nothing seems impossible, and you intuitively seek perfection. You feel connected to something larger than your immediate task. You look up from your work to see that the day's flown past. You approach your work like an artist approaches the canvas, a songwriter the keyboard, a sculptor the marble block. Hit that zone, and you *become* an artist.

Zoning Out

You know it when you're a misfit. Everything is a bore and a chore. The day drags on in dismal drudgery and stifling mediocrity. On a bad day you think about sabotage—to others, to the company. You live for the raise or promotion. You get better at what you do, but for reasons of advancement only. You ravage your creative energy in the constant search for something more or better. If it comes along, you snatch it without batting an eye. You've got no skin in the game—no commitment, no connection.

The reality is that no one hits their zone all day, every day. You're always somewhere between the two poles. But if you're not constantly angling to position your ability to more fully *connect to the task*, engagement—and thus ingenuity—will remain always out of reach.

Cause: All Intents & Purposes

It's easy to lose sight of the meaning behind your work when you're part of a large organization. But that's the second point of connection: the *cause* you're fighting for. It's a higher level of fit. Miss it, and you won't be able to dig your own job.

FYI

The Gallup Organization estimates that 20% of workers in America are simply not engaged fully in their work, including over 22 million "actively disengaged."

Walk into any Toyota operation, and you'll see that everyone is in sync with the same aim: highest quality, lowest cost, shortest lead time . . . *for your particular customer.* Everything is tied to that singular purpose.

Most companies do an annual dance around

purpose, spending days in offsites to conduct what amounts to a creative writing exercise in which they draft pithy statements meant to inspire, but that inevitably ring hollow and fail to capture the real reason they exist. That's why they do it every year...they're still trying to get it right.

> *A man has got to know his limitations.*
> **Clint Eastwood,**
> in *Dirty Harry*

And we're no better at the individual level. We're great at titles and describing what we do. We're lousy at pinpointing exactly why we do it.

But here's the thing: *cause* trumps *task*. Because when you've connected at the higher level, you know you're making a difference. *Helping people.* And that's the most powerful motivator there is. You could be in the job you're born for, but if you're fuzzy on the significance of it in the grand scheme of things, you'll disconnect. There goes your ingenuity.

The good news is that cause is fairly easy to discover, regardless of whether at the company or individual level.

Form Following Function

We get caught up in the form our work takes—job titles, occupations, careers. *I'm in sales, I'm an attorney, I'm a writer.* Those are merely convenient descriptions of activity. They can block us from seeing the importance of our work, our *function.*

For those struggling to make the connection, a simple technique called *The 5 Whys* can help. Toyota uses the method to discover the root cause of a problem, but it can be used to discover personal cause as well. Here's how it works: Start with any job description. *I'm a census taker; I collect nationwide household information and compile thorough reports.* Then it's a matter of peeling the onion. *Why is that important?* Because it gives the government current information on our nation's population. *Why is that important?* Because we can then understand our population trends. *Why is that important?* Because it helps our government make informed decisions. *Why is that important?* Because it enables the government to improve the social welfare of the nation. And there's the cause: *improving the welfare of the nation.*

Paul Guitierrez*

New United Motor Manufacturing

He is a career autoworker working at the GM/Toyota joint venture plant located in Fremont, California.

Never in a million years would I tell you this work is creative. Then Toyota took over twenty years ago. They teach us their system then say to us, "we want you to tell us how to make it better." We went from "just do your job" with GM to "no one knows the job better than you" with Toyota. They teach us how to solve problems. They turn us loose in here! They say, stop the line anytime if something's wrong. I was floored. They think I can make their systems better? They're giving me the power to stop production? That right there changed my life. All of a sudden, I'm looking for ways to fix problems, make improvements, basically get rid of anything that was stupid. Get rid of waste, they said. Perfect the operation, they said. So now all of a sudden I'm using my head, I'm the expert, I'm creating new procedures. There you go, creating. I guess there's an art to it, yeah. It's not like I carved a Corolla or anything, but I started getting some real pride back. Before, we didn't care, we were ashamed to say where we worked. We'd laugh when we saw a car that came out of here. Now we feel like, hey, I built that! The place got cleaned up. We stopped fighting. We all wore the same uniforms, even managers. We started thinking, hey, people are driving these cars, let's make them safe. My mark's all over this plant, like everyone else's. One year we did like eight thousand ideas. The job itself wasn't creative, never will be, but our job was to *be* creative. And I guess if you can be creative in this line of work, you can be creative anywhere.

*A pseudonym.

The beauty of understanding cause is that it frees you to accept a wider variety of jobs, because you can remain true to your cause regardless of the form your work takes. Form follows function!

By getting to the bottom of the simple question—*Why is my work important?*—managers will see their cause as helping people improve their performance, not just running a department. Autoworkers will come to see their job as protecting families as they travel, not just operating machinery. A coffee counterperson will view her work as not just serving coffee but rather helping busy people get a nice start to a hectic day. A golf course greenskeeper will see his work not as lawn maintenance, but a creative challenge to enable golfers to shoot their best round.

Now *that's* art. And that's just *Side A* of the ingenuity coin.

Side B: Exploration

Call it tinkering. Or testing. Or tweaking. Whatever you call it, it's the enemy of the status quo, of complacency, and of the ordinary. Want to work like an artist? *New* and *better* is your creed. Because for the artist, *as is* just isn't acceptable.

So it's not enough to be technically proficient at something. Sure, to be a true master at anything, one must first gain command of old-school methods. But competence and workmanship is just the ante to the game. Ingenuity is about new, better, different. We all marvel at the wizards who not only perform the basics to near perfection, but then actually change the game and achieve hero status: Larry Page and Sergey Brin (Google founders), Steve Jobs (Apple Computer), Ted Turner (Turner Broadcasting), Frederick Smith (Federal Express), Walt Disney (animation), Lance Armstrong (cycling), Jake Burton (snowboarding), Dick Fosbury (high-jumping).

Art Works

Art has its foundations in utility. Great works of earlier centuries were never meant to hang in museums and adorn private collections any more than elegant Egyptian hieroglyphics were meant to simply beautify crypts, wooden totem poles to garnish the forest, or coarse images of the hunter's kill to decorate the walls of a cave.

Rather, they were intended for a very specific purpose or to signify a specific event, judged first and foremost by function and usefulness, and by the ability to meet the requirements of the commissioner.

They were made by people, *for* people.

Julie Marken*

Starbucks

**She is a part-time employee and college student.
We chat during her break.**

This is definitely coffee art. But if you think people are buying coffee, you're wrong. There's something going on here more like a caffeine cult...the same people come in every day, even though they have plenty of options. After a while, you get to know people. You talk to them, you learn about them, maybe what they do, or what their kids' names are. You want to know more. There's a little bond built. You start to figure out that they look forward to coming here for reasons other than the buzz. They like the familiarity...they like knowing you know their name, that you remember their favorite drink. Our team is like a little family, and they like that. We have fun, and they like that. Energizes them, lifts them. You can see it. There's a kind of funky trust thing going on. You know how you talk to the bartender or your hair stylist? That sort of thing. It's funny, you get a certain sense of pride working here that you don't get other places. I know, I've worked in them. And that makes you want to do your job the best you can. More so, even. Make it better if you can. I'm just part-time, I'm in school part-time, I want to be a journalist. But I've learned a lot about people being here. It's going to make me a better writer, interviewer, I think. Not everyone feels this way, but I feel like I'm providing really busy people a nice start to a hectic day in a safe little getaway. We're picking people up, or perking them up.
[smiles] Pun intended. It's not just a coffee shop, and it's not about the coffee.

*A pseudonym.

We're talking about the application of imagination here. And the key ingredient is constant exploration.

To do it, you have to accept and respect the limitations of your specific medium—like any artist—and pursue possibility within the given confines, leveraging the constraints to drive new ideas and methods. That's a mindshift for most. But eight basic notes in music doesn't seem to have stifled the ingenuity of musicians.

And you have to intensely and relentlessly pursue the kinds of questions found at the heart of most every breakthrough, big or small. The kind that always drive new-school thinking: *Is there a better way, a different way? What's possible, given my abilities?*

Wondering About

Exploration always starts with a question. And the right question is far more important than the right answer. Author Milan Kundera once said, *"I ask questions. The stupidity of people comes from having an answer for everything. The wisdom of the novel comes from having a question for everything."*

The problem is that we forget how to ask questions, starting at around age five. That's when childlike curiosity begins to fade. That's when the formal, systematic indoctrination into the ritual of accumulating knowledge begins. But what we know is dwarfed by what we don't, so if we want to actually know *more*, it seems a little strange to focus only on the known. We've lost the ability of a four-year-old to ask questions. Lots of them. Most of them dumb. So we spend our lives learning all the right answers—the ones we're being spoon-fed—instead of chasing the right questions. Then we sit back and ask why we don't get any smarter.

The answer is that we breed conformity of thought. And suppress curiosity. We're often so

New-School Rules

#1: Question everything. Then do it again.

#2: Start every conversation with a question. Even if the conversation is with yourself.

#3: Answer every question with a question.

#4: Ask at least one dumb question in every meeting.

#5: Begin every idea, recommendation, or suggestion as a question.

#6: Have three questions you always ask someone.

#7: Develop the single question that drives your work.

Do the same thing for your life.

adamant about what we know and believe to be true that we limit ourselves to only the options right in front of us, and fail to consider what's truly *possible*.

Everything we know now was at one time undiscovered. So it makes sense to make discovery a major part of the daily work.

Ingenuity is all about the right question. The question is everything. The *question* is the real muse.

TILTING AT DRAGONS: THE HARD WORK OF ART

One needs a bit of storybook hero in them to tackle the obstacles to ingenuity. And there are plenty of them. You hear it in the whines of the seemingly put-upon: *Our culture is too bureaucratic. My ideas don't count. I don't get the resources I need.* And, of course, the all-time most popular refrain of the uninspired, heard on front lines and in boardrooms alike: *My boss won't let me.*

That's victimism, which at Toyota is a career-stunting choice. It's the polar opposite of leadership. Leaders choose to control their own destiny. Like any other company, Toyota fields its fair share of victims. Toyota's robust approach to problem solving simply fosters more leaders at every level pursuing ideas they know will move the company forward.

Slaying dragons and storming castles isn't for the faint of heart. The root meaning of ingenuity means *free thinker.* In a world run by powerful bosses and inflexible systems, rarely if ever is creative license granted freely. It's *taken.* And that takes basic courage. Or at least a soldier's bravado. It's the obstacles that make the achievement so impressive. If it was easy, we wouldn't be talking about it. No challenge, no creativity.

Even the most oppressive maximum security prison in the world fosters creative thinking—albeit about escape. So avoid the pity pot at all costs. *Use* the rejection, *use* the system, *use* the constraints, and *use* the Machiavellian boss to your creative advantage. Those are tremendous forces working against you. Redirect them to fuel your imagination. Challenge yourself. Reframe the problem.

It's never easy, but it *can* be done. Two stories prove the point...one old, one new.

Shanghai Design

The Power of the Question

At least one person doesn't think "Chinese fashion design" is an oxymoron. Young artist-turned-designer Lu Kun has almost single-handedly put Shanghai on the international fashion map by pursuing three questions: *Why doesn't China's clothing industry pay attention to detail? Why is it so cheap and uninspired? Why can't we do it differently?*

Tired of his country being perceived as one big factory, Kun is on a mission to demonstrate that creativity and innovation are alive and well in China. His bold designs are doing just that. Drawing his inspiration from what he knows best—the streets of Shanghai—Kun's original creations are being hailed as elegant and imaginative, yet at the same time distinctly Shanghainese.

Undaunted by China's lack of a financial backing system for developing promising fashion designers, Kun has broken new ground. Until the arrival of Mr. Lu, no Chinese designer has achieved a presence on the international catwalk.

Kun's done it in less than five years.

It's as if Mr. Lu took the advice of Sakichi Toyoda, who said: *"Never try to design something without first gaining at least three years hands-on experience."* Kun's path to innovation? Learning the basics of fashion design in a vocational high school. One year of cutting and sewing at a Shanghai tailor shop. One year at a startup Hong Kong label. One year teaching sewing technique and production design at LaSalle International Fashion School in Shanghai. Then out on his own as a personal fashion designer for wealthy individuals. And finally the design of an entire line of special occasion and upscale casual wear.

As with all great innovators, questions drive Kun's artistry.

The Artist and the Pope

The legend bears retelling of the stormy relationship between sculptor Michelangelo and his "manager," Pope Julius II. The Pope dreamed of a grand mausoleum for himself, and commissioned Michelangelo, who proposed an ambitious concept of more than forty marble statues. Design approved, the jubilant Michelangelo spent nearly a year in the hills cutting massive marble blocks. But the Pope's advisors viewed Michelangelo as a threat to their influence, and convinced Julius to end the project before it began. Michelangelo was outraged. On advice of counsel, Julius then challenged Michelangelo to paint the Sistine Chapel *al fresco*.

> For painters, composers, or sculptors, creating involves working within the constraints imposed by media. If one had but to snap one's fingers and the vision became reality, there would be no creative process.
>
> **Peter Senge**

It was a diabolical scheme. The Pope's advisors knew that Michelangelo not only detested painting as a medium, but further had no experience whatsoever with fresco. If Michelangelo accepted the commission, the anticipated failure would easily rank his work inferior to that of painter Raphael, who was being hailed a genius. The comparison would destroy Michelangelo. If he refused, his career would end that day. Michelangelo protested, even suggesting Raphael for the job. To no avail. He had no choice.

So Michelangelo did what a true artist does. He summoned his grit, sacrificed self, and served his commissioner.

He took artistic license, using the adverse situation to drive his creativity, channeling his passionate anger into the work. He refused the help of expert fresco painters brought in to advise, and completely reinvented fresco technique. He expanded the job, deciding to paint the walls as well. He built his own scaffolding, locked himself in the chapel, and for four years contorted himself, hanging upside down, painting the incredible scenes.

Michelangelo was quoted as saying: "If people knew how hard I worked to get my mastery, it wouldn't seem so wonderful after all."

The rest is history. And a powerful lesson in the art of ingenuity.

Rx for Deadly Mistakes

When design student Deborah Adler's grandma Helen took Grandpa Herman's prescription medication Amoxicillin by mistake in 2001, it was a signal for Deborah to apply her skills and make sure such a thing never happened again. Coming from a family of doctors, the world of medicine was a familiar one. When the unfortunate accident occurred, it became clear to Deborah that she had an opportunity to develop an idea that both hit close to home and satisfied her need to help others.

A single question drove her pursuit of a new design: **How can I make medicine bottles more safe and user-friendly?**

She immersed herself in the problem, exploiting her own need for an MFA thesis project at New York's School of Visual Arts. She discovered that people take medication incorrectly 60% of the time. Grandma Helen's problem was almost universal.

Medication bottles hadn't changed much in 60 years. Sure, there was child-proofing in the 1970s. But simple observation told a story of deadly complexity: Inconsistent labeling. Confusing numbers. Poor color combinations. Hard-to-read shape. Tiny type, except for the drugstore's name and logo.

Her goals? Clarity. Visibility. Intuitiveness. Personalization. The new design included turning the bottle upside down and flattening it, so the label doesn't wrap out of view. The prescription information is delivered in a hierarchy of priority, starting with the medication in big bold letters. Back label directions (e.g., "Take with food") are standardized and icon-based. Information cards tuck neatly into the back of the bottle label. Color-coded rings make it hard to take the wrong medication, because every family member has their own designated color.

Target liked it so much that they bought up her patent rights and fast-tracked the design to all 1000-plus Target pharmacies nationwide, dubbing it Clear Rx.

The Clear Rx design is a true work of art. So much so that the New York Museum of Modern Art put it on display in the autumn of 2005.

The Prince and the Gazoo

Toyota is not immune to the political ails afflicting big companies. And bureaucracy can indeed kill ideas. But only if you let it. The story of Akio Toyoda, the great-grandson of Sakichi Toyoda, tells the tale.

You'd think the young scion would have a fairly easy time getting his ideas heard and approved, and that a member of the founding family would be given special consideration and comparatively free reign. Not necessarily. In fact, his ideas might not have survived but for his courage and personal leadership.

Akio Toyoda joined Toyota in the mid-1980s, and for the next ten years occupied himself with a single question: *Why don't we apply our lean manufacturing approach to our distribution system?*

In what amounted to a full frontal attack on dealership efficiency, Akio's early efforts failed dismally at the hands of a powerful distribution system, owing mostly to his blatant disregard for the established structure. Undaunted but lesson learned, he took a new approach by cultivating a handful of loyal lieutenants from engineering posts and launching the Office of Business Revolution Promotion, the express aim of which was to streamline workflow in Toyota's Japan dealerships. A large distribution center was the first target. For six months Akio and his team put in 100-hour weeks and lived in a cheap hotel. Results were impressive: Delivery time to dealers was cut from a week to three days.

> *Why does it take a factory just 20 to 30 hours to make a car, but it takes 40-plus days for a dealer to deliver and get paid for one?*
>
> **Akio Toyoda**

Akio's legacy was born. In 1995, Toyota leadership shifted to a non-family member for the first time in thirty years. Chairman Shoichiro Toyoda, Akio's father, appointed Hiroshi Okuda as president. The head-butting began almost immediately, and Akio found himself fighting harder and longer than most to create meaningful change.

But like any business artist, his path was lit by questions. That year, the question tugging at Akio was: *Do Japanese prefer conservative white cars, which Toyota pumps out in huge numbers, or flashier colors? What if what the customer really wants is a red Corolla?*

And so began Akio's quest to somehow link up Toyota's dealers to share information on customers. As serendipity would have it, Akio met the head of Microsoft's Japan unit, and posed the very question.

Microsoft's suggestion was to use an emerging technology called the World Wide Web to answer those kinds of questions and share information quickly and cheaply.

Within a year, Akio's team launched Gazoo.com. The site linked dealers and customers, and offered all kinds of information on new and used vehicles, as well as innovative features like a virtual body shop for dealers to offer repair quotes.

The concept was nearly dead on arrival. Dealers and executives alike opposed it, fearful that it would somehow steal dealers' sales. Only Fujio Cho, Akio's mentor and presently vice chairman, favored the idea. With a tiny budget, Akio began operations.

The powers that be did everything they could to squash Gazoo.com. They banned advertising on television, radio, and print. Akio's response was to use guerrilla tactics. Exploit a loophole in the ban: *trains*. Akio outsmarted the opposition by plastering posters in every depot.

It wasn't long before Gazoo.com caught on with consumers. The site is now a full-feature e-commerce destination supported by multimedia kiosks in dealerships and convenience stores all over Japan. Books, DVDs, travel reservations, and financial services all contribute to the multibillion-dollar annual revenue.

> **Toyota's Gazoo.com Wins Kudos for Embracing the New Economy**
> *Wall Street Journal* headline
> August 28, 2000

And Akio? A seat on Toyota's Board of Directors!

THE PRICE OF ART

The search for elegant solutions begins with the principle of *ingenuity in craft*. And ingenuity is not about artistic ability or invention or deliberately trying to think of big ideas. It's less a talent than a way of operating. A behavior. That means you can learn it, develop it, and perfect it.

It starts with what's right in front of you. The daily work. Artists and scientists dig their own job, so they own the work. Their world revolves around masterful work performed for worthy reasons toward a meaningful end. They go their own way in the face of what to most looks to be impossible. The ability to do so triggers the magic, the alchemy. That's art.

It's a different mindset, and anything different is risky. And most certainly a form of leadership. So there's a penalty for it. Criticism. Denial. Rejection. Dismissal. Laughter.

Whatsoever you write, or paint, or play, or sing, or build, no one will strive to surpass or to slander you unless your work be stamped with the seal of genius.

Theodore McManus

New-school wizards know they'll face pushback from the old-school skeptics, but they trust the knowledge and skill they've developed through building on their key abilities, continuing to employ their ingenuity to explore and experiment with new ways of doing things. They view defeat as the chance to begin again.

So expect it. And ignore it. Keep on tinkering, tailoring, and trying. And don't expect big rewards. Don't expect anyone to beat a path to your door to embrace your ideas. Don't expect anyone to help or support you.

Do it so you can look at yourself in the mirror every day with pride. That's the biggest and best payoff.

Whatever your work, make it your art, your canvas, and your sandbox. All sorts of good things happen when you do.

REFLECTION

What opportunities exist to dig your own job?

How well do you connect with your task?

Why is your work important?

What questions are you pursuing?

When have you been the right person with the right idea?

CHAPTER 2

The Pursuit of Perfection

The artist ought never allow anything to overcome his sense of the main end of art—perfection.
Michelangelo

A Discipline of Increments

If ingenuity is the starting point in the search for elegant solutions, it needs a worthy aim, one that will point us toward the most important opportunities.

Perfection best fits the bill. It's the highest standard of excellence, the ideal. It's a worthy aim, so it seems reasonable to think that it's the one ultimate goal universally embraced and chased.

It's not. The world is getting spanked by poor quality. Which means the spreading blaze of personal artistry is somehow being doused by a more powerful or prevalent force: *mediocrity*. Getting it right has been replaced by getting it out. With a few striking exceptions, industry seems to have bought into the lie that given quality, cost, and speed, you can have two, but not all three. Speed and cost we have down cold. A new gadget, with more doohickeys than we know what to do with, will come out tomorrow. Meanwhile, we still can't figure out how to use what we bought today. More important, it doesn't work so well. Your cell phone takes pictures, sends messages, records video, and plays music. But the main function, making calls, is...just okay.

The most disturbing part is that we've accepted it. Companies have learned that customers will tolerate schlock, wait for the new model, buy it, and toss the old one. But the new one's no better. Just cheaper and more complex. It's become a way of life.

Who cares? Companies like Toyota, Apple, Gore, GE. They keep the flame alive and reap the rewards. For Toyota, there is simply no other choice. Perfection is always, always the target.

Perfection demands a discipline, one focused on increments and details that carry huge impact. But here's why that's so hard.

CAN'T GET NO SATISFACTION

Elegant solutions demand optimizing quality, cost, and speed. They're the three primary *tangible* drivers of customer value in all goods and services. Taken together, they separate the leaders from the followers. Optimization is all about reaching high for the ideal. It requires relentless vigil and an eye for detail. It demands a strong discipline aimed at perfecting all three, because the tension created by imperfection fuels true innovation at any level.

Here's the rub: we're just not that good at it.

The annual American Customer Satisfaction Index shows a broad decline in consumer sentiment over the last ten years. Computers down over 5%. Major appliances down nearly 6%. Airlines down 8%. Telecommunications down 13%. Information, television, news, down 16%. Even some of the A-list companies are lagging. Dell, Hewlett-Packard, AT&T, Nokia, Marriott. What's on the rise? The old school: automobiles. Who's at the top? Toyota.

The numbers don't reveal the worst part. Firms have learned to profit from poor quality. Not only is warranty expense now built into many business models, it's become a hefty revenue stream. So you can build junk, sell the extended warranty, and when the thing breaks, you replace it, then fix it and sell it again as— get this—*new*. Some electronics makers have become savvy double-dippers in just this way. Sure, the better brands shun the practice. Their products still outlive the warranty. But the also-rans? Expect their stuff to fail on expiration day. In the long run, that hurts. It hurts customers, and it hurts the brand.

> *Quality is never an accident; it is always the result of high intention, sincere effort, intelligent direction, and skillful execution.*
> **William A. Foster**

Quality is on the endangered species list. The pursuit of perfection is something only a noble few choose to do. But it's the *right* thing to do.

And it's the pathway to elegant solutions.

Fishing for Red Herring

Perfection generally gets a bum rap. Blame it on the temptations—swinging for fences, getting too clever, and solving problems frivolously. The pressure to show short-term rapid growth makes them irresistible to all but the shrewdest innovators. They divert attention from what the real work should be. They make it hard to see the path clearly.

Pundits don't make it any easier. Nearly every tome on the topic makes a big deal about the big idea. That's understandable, because dramatic, high visibility leaps in performance are newsworthy. Big ideas draw the spotlight, which makes the pundit's job of investigating and theorizing based on observable effect that much easier. They don't have to spend the enormous amount of time it takes to understand the nuances of the intricate process behind the innovation.

They unwittingly discount the power of the everyday innovation admittedly short on sex appeal, and dismiss it with words that have taken on a subordinate, nearly negative connotation: *continuous, incremental, evolutionary improvement,* versus the ever more desirable *radical, disruptive, revolutionary innovation.*

There's a double standard at play. In one corner we have the marketers whose ad copy trumpets the tiniest tweak to a product as a groundbreaking innovation. In the other corner we have the scholars and sages who constantly whisper in the CEO's ear that large-scale innovation is all that really matters. In fairness, both perspectives place growth as the foremost consideration.

But every good idea represents a breakthrough on some level. Magnitude is a red herring of the first order. Here's why.

> **Perspective**
>
> You'd have to double your top line to equal the impact on the bottom line of small process improvements that save 10% of costs. And that's not even including the huge investment you'd have to make up front to design, develop, and test a new product or service that will grow revenue 100%.
>
> It's the innovations aimed at the bottom line that yield the profits to fund investment in new products and services.

1. The Da Vinci Dilemma

Leonardo da Vinci was never at a loss for big ideas. Brilliant, ingenious ideas centuries before their time filled the pages of his legendary notebooks. And that's where they remained. Until the innovators in another lifetime took them and shaped them into something actually workable.

History continues to repeat the lesson. Apple Computer didn't dream up the whole mouse and icon system interface, Xerox did. Apple made it a commercially viable concept. They stuck with it, continued to perfect it, and produced a truly elegant solution.

Turn-the-world-upside-down ideas rarely if ever work as originally conceived. Are they valuable? Of course. The point is that without the process of perfection that makes them useful, the gap between the idea and the application is so wide that people don't get it. They resist it, so the invention remains a novel brainstorm. Until you scale it back and scope it down. Sculpt it and hone it into something more manageable, acceptable, and useful.

And the big earth-shattering ideas are few and far between. They have huge lead times. They have enormous carrying costs. You absolutely need them to pepper the advance into new eras of industry. But for the mainstream business that seeks to achieve and sustain continuous success through steady progress, the real power of innovation lives in the minor tremors—the more plentiful and more immediately actionable smaller ideas.

2. Evolution & Eureka

Charles Darwin was on to something. Business innovation has a lot in common with his evolution theory on the origin of species.

First there's the notion that everything can be traced to a common ancestry; that is, every idea has elements of the past. Take the Toyota Production System. It's part Henry Ford's assembly line, part grocery store inventory system, and part automatic loom mechanics. And Henry Ford's assembly line? Continuous flow borrowed from mills and canning factories; standardized parts borrowed from machine tooling; conveyor belts borrowed from meatpacking and brewing industries.

Second is the idea of similar traits converging into one new organism. That's TiVo. Recipe: one part computer, one part *TV Guide*, one part video recorder—mix and stir. It's cellular phones and PDAs, which now combine telephony, text messaging, email, Internet browsing, voice recording, mp3 music, video, and photography. It's the convergence of cellular and wireless Voice Over Internet Protocol technology in the next wave of dual mode cell phones, an innovation likely to significantly change both the industry and consumer usage.

> *I invented nothing new. I simply assembled into a car the discoveries of other men behind whom were centuries of work.*
> **Henry Ford**

Third is survival of the fittest, which says failure to make small adaptations leads to extinction. Take the removable storage media industry. It went from 5.25-inch to 3.5-inch drives, then to Zip, CD, DVD, and thumb drives. Many of the leading firms died out, because they failed to adopt newer technology that customers wanted.

All of which is to say, there's not much new under the sun. Most of the so-called revolutionary breakthroughs—the mythical *eureka!* moments—are in reality smaller ideas combined, synthesized, and adapted to a new application. It's nearly impossible to find a big innovation that isn't based on something else already in existence. Microsoft knows that better than anyone. Nearly every product they've ever sold is borrowed, bought, or built, on something designed previously.

So that's reason enough to repurpose some of the energy you've earmarked for landing the big one. It's all about evolution.

3. Dissing the Ground Game

The pursuit of perfection gets no respect. Most firms consider it to be more trouble than it's worth. They sell short the balanced portfolio power generated by a large and steady stream of smaller scale ideas in favor of the hunt for killer apps. That's a mistake for the same reason you "don't put all your eggs in one basket" by investing every dollar in a single stock, as economist James Tobin advised in his 1981 Nobel Prize–winning thesis on portfolio selection and diversification. It leaves you at the mercy of the market with no hedge against the bet. It's risky and foolhardy.

Everything New Is Old

The vast majority of ideas considered revolutionary are actually much more evolutionary than you might think.

In airports and hotels, you can now buy high-ticket items like iPODs, cell phone accessories, and digital cameras from vending machines. Radical new idea? The practice has been commonplace in Japan for years. And high-dollar vending machines? Think ATMs—vending machines for cash. Vending machines are actually 2000 years old. Greek scientist Hero built a contraption that would release holy water when a coin fell on a lever that opened a valve.

Leonardo da Vinci's notebooks reveal ancestral sketches of ideas implemented centuries later: Crane. Submarine. Life preserver. Helicopter. Parachute. Scuba. Skates. Hand grenade.

Recognizing that John Fitch and James Rumsey invented the steamboat 20 years earlier, Robert Fulton, credited with the innovation, said: "Although the [water] wheels are not a new application, if I combine them in such a way that a large proportion of the power of the engine acts to propel the boat in the same way as if the purchase was upon the ground, the combination will be better than anything that has been done up to the present and it is in fact a new discovery."

Hockey great Wayne Gretsky's innovative behind-the-goal techniques were borrowed from the game of lacrosse, a sport French explorers based on a game the Cherokee and Iroquois used to prepare for battle.

Email is a combination of two existing applications, one written for a computer to send messages to itself, the other written to enable two computers to communicate.

Bob Dylan created a new music genre by simply combining folk and rock. As for rock, it is rhythm and blues with an up-tempo backbeat and country chord progression.

USC's innovative spread-option offense resulting in 34 straight wins beginning in 2003 is a simple hybrid of the spread and the option offenses that have been around for several decades.

The calculator can be traced to Blaise Pascal, who in 1642 designed a mechanical addition and subtraction machine.

All of the following are in fact based substantially on a preexisting product or service: World Wide Web; Southwest Air; JetBlue; light beer; FedEx; New Beetle; disposable diapers; cellular phones; Big Bertha Driver; digital watch; online banking; ballpoint pen; and yes, eBay (think flea markets).

The first problem is that continuous improvement happened to be one of a flurry of quality efforts in the mid-1990s, which all flamed out for the same reason: the silver bullet syndrome, aka, magic pills for business ills. They were trounced out as the new program, and neither embraced as a serious discipline nor internalized. Consequently, there was no deep learning, and no new capability built. Managers wanted excellence, but didn't want to put the hard work in. They wanted cheap, quick hits to show results. It was a reactionary stance focused on compliance and correction, on fixing defects, not a search for the ideal or optimal way to do something. They failed to build a necessary critical mass of more proactive and forward-looking individual and team projects. They held out continuous improvement as something separate from innovation. When the low-hanging fruit was picked clean, and the painstaking work of instilling a true system-wide routine for finding and solving tougher problems began, they went searching for a new silver bullet.

Another problem is reporting. Innovation is covered either as a groundbreaking event of rare genius or a fortunate accident. Fulton's steamboat. Edison's lightbulb. Whitney's cotton gin. Case studies of everything from penicillin to Post-its perpetuate the misconception. The painful process behind the breakthrough is neglected. The stories are all about the master stroke, the final outcome, and the strategic implications.

So we're still clueless on the rigors of constant innovation. In the end, successful organizational systems and structures get mislabeled as strong culture, something pundits love to preach. So the resulting advice runs along the lines of (all apologies to The Youngbloods): *C'mon people now, let's get creative. Everybody get together, try to do something better right now.*

Good luck with that.

The pursuit of perfection must be *disciplinary,*

Chasing Toyota

There's a simple explanation for why Toyota's success is hard to replicate. Their system drives a universal focus on ground-level innovation, to the point that the pursuit of perfection is part of who they are, not just what they do.

Toyota's factory floor associates might implement over a dozen ideas per shift. Managers might spend over half their time on a portfolio of ideas and projects.

So by the time a competitor has observed, lifted, and installed a certain method, Toyota is already doing it differently.

And better than it's ever been done before.

not programmatic. It can't be relegated to a department. It can't be reserved for top-level management. It can't be just about eliminating defects. It must be the creative core to the daily work of everyone in the organization, not a sideline event or activity. It must be about progress. It must be universally understood to be the path to a future everyone has a stake in. You have to *own* it.

That kind of discipline requires a fundamental mindshift. That's what makes it so very, very hard. *There is no easy way.* Most of us will count ourselves lucky if we get the chance to understand and practice the pursuit of perfection. Because it happens only over time and through experience. You have to do it over and over again to get it. At Toyota, that's not luck. They make sure of that. In Toyota's view, a million smaller ideas trumps a single big breakthrough any day of the week.

The pursuit of perfection *is* the work.

GETTING TO THE CHASE

Perspective

Pursuing perfection is something everyone has experienced.

Anyone who has ever arranged flowers in a vase, decorated a Christmas tree, wrestled with a stubborn hairdo, or fretted over a wardrobe ensemble, knows something of the creative struggle to get everything just right.

A splash of red here, more tinsel there, an extra tease for good measure—the process is one of inching your way to the perfect proportions: adding and adjusting, mixing and matching, tinkering and tailoring to make it just so...and the littlest changes can make all the difference.

Toyota pursues perfection by starting with the ideal, then working backward, removing anything that stands in the way. That means looking at the target in a fundamentally different way. It means asking *what's blocking perfection?* instead of *what can we improve?* That's what differentiates their brand of continuous improvement from all others.

So what does the pursuit of perfection look like? The best way to bring it to life in a meaningful way is through the compelling story of Lexus, Toyota's luxury brand that has become the *de facto* embodiment of the endless pursuit of perfection.

The secret luxury vehicle project under development by Toyota in the mid-1980s was codenamed F1, for "flagship one." The mission was impossible: beat BMW and Mercedes-Benz at their own game. That meant besting both in comfort, styling, performance, handling, noise, aerodynamics, weight, and fuel efficiency. It meant putting every element under the microscope. It meant six years, 1400 designers, 3700 engineers, 900 engine prototypes, 450 test models. And nearly two million test miles.

When the LS400 made its debut in 1989, it stunned the automotive world and set a new luxury standard. The facts made history: in every category rated by *Car & Driver*, the LS400 trumped the best of the best: BMW 735i and Mercedes 420SEL. The Lexus LS400 was five decibels quieter, 120 pounds lighter, 17 miles per hour faster, got more than four more miles to the gallon, and retailed for $30,000 less than the BMW 735i.

Here's how it happened.

The timing couldn't have been better when in the summer of 1983 Toyota Chairman Eiji Toyoda issued the challenge to build the best car in the world. The company had seen twenty years of steadily improving market share on U.S. soil culminate in nearly a decade as the leading import. A significant share of Toyota customers had moved up in class and wealth and were searching for a vehicle to match their status.

Building the best car in the world meant dethroning the kings of luxury: BMW, Mercedes, Jaguar, and Cadillac. But the venture wasn't as crazy as it sounded. Luxury and performance wasn't completely uncharted territory. Toyota built limousines for executives and dignitaries. Toyota engineers worked on World War II fighter jets. Toyota had competed in motorsports for over a quarter century.

In Toyota's view, they weren't building a car, they were redefining perfection. The goal demanded a perfect plan; anything less would leave them short of the target. No amount of execution acumen would make up for a solid strategy. The plan would take six months, but the decision was clear: start clean. Design the car from the ground up. It was the only way. Nothing in the current stable was even close to the class of car needed.

> Now it is time to build a car that is better than the best in the world.
> **Eiji Toyoda,** 1983

The first step was to assemble the A team. Shoji Jimbo, master designer of Celica and Cressida fame, was chosen as the chief engineer. Needing the best behind him, creative leaders willing to unshackle themselves from the conserva-

tive Japanese styling, Jimbo recruited Ichiro Suzuki for the body structure and Kunihiro Uchida for the exterior design. Suzuki wanted to hire Akihiro "Dezi" Nagaya, a kid still in design school who thought cars were sculptures that just happened to move. By October 1984 the team was in place.

The second step was to identify the target. To do so, the team needed to grasp the situation and understand the competition. The decision was made to escape the confines of the corporate environment and begin to formulate ideas. They decided that the only way to truly get a bead on the competition was to drive the hundred forty-plus miles out to the countryside near Fujiyama, each team member taking separate cars, each renting a member of the competitive set: BMW, Mercedes, Cadillac, Jaguar, Audi, Volvo. It worked. The targets were unanimously identified: Mercedes S class and BMW 7 series. They were the best of the best, and true icons.

Step three was to understand the customer, to get inside the hearts and minds of American luxury buyers, to learn the ways of luxury, to understand the values. The decision is made in 1985 to take the team to Southern California and live the lifestyle, where a beachfront house in Laguna Beach would be the team's quarters for several months.

The house was actually part of the research. It was also close to Toyota's Newport Beach design center, Calty Design Research, where the car would be designed. Chief designer Dennis Campbell and Toyota designer Michikazu Masu, on assignment at Calty, would have major roles.

A tour of the luxury lifestyle became the centerpiece of study, including expensive malls, tony restaurants, country clubs, trendy nightclubs, and designer boutiques. Valets, caddies, chauffeurs, and caterers were queried to find out druthers of the upper crust. The team continued their competitive study by leasing Mercedeses, BMWs, Porsches, and Jaguars. Similar tours of San Francisco, Miami, New York City, Houston, Denver, and Chicago were conducted. The luxury scene was a whole new world for the team. Only criminals in Japan lived that way.

To bolster the observations, anthropologists, psychologists, and focus groups weighed in. The research showed that luxury-car owners bought image, quality, resale value, performance, and safety, in that order.

Quality, resale, and safety are right up Toyota's alley. That performance is down on the list is a surprise, and a key opportunity. But the biggest hurdle for Toyota would be image.

In August 1985, all but five of the core team returned to Japan, and the real work began. Image and performance became the top two objectives.

Back in Japan, engineers had begun dismantling the top-end BMWs and Mercedeses, laying out every part and keeping only the best as the minimally accepted standard.

Meanwhile in Newport Beach, deciding what the car would look like was the first order of business. Uchida took three concepts back to Japan, all of which were panned universally. It's the first of many, many failures. The rejection centers on the aggressive styling: it's not bland enough, and too American. The American team was stunned, knowing conservatism won't cut it. But it's back to the drawing board for more sketches and more clay models.

> You cannot create a 'child of America' unless you understand Americans. What does a car mean to them? How do they use it? How do they feel when they ride in a car?
>
> **Yukiyasu Togo,** President Toyota Motor Sales, 1983

Round two was rejected as well, so Uchida began going back and forth to Japan nearly every month with revised sketches and models. By the end of 1986, there was still no resolution on what the car would look like.

As 1987 began, Jimbo would get promoted and name Ichiro Suzuki, chief body structure engineer, as his replacement. It's a new regime, and Suzuki laid down the law. Perfection demands a perfectionist. There would be no compromises, no derivatives, and nothing Japanese about the car. Suzuki fixed his vision on luxury and performance, and set the bar high. The car must best, not match, the BMW 735i in all performance measures. It must be faster, quieter, lighter, easier to handle, more comfortable, and more fuel efficient.

The BMW 735i had a top speed of 138 mph, got 19 mpg, had an aerodynamic drag of .32, a sound level of 61 dB at 60 mph, and weighed 3880 pounds. The Mercedes 420SE trailed ever so slightly in all areas, but was the import sales leader in the United States. Beating Mercedes in sales volume would signal success. Suzuki's vision: Top speed, 155 mph. Fuel efficiency, over 22.5 mpg. Coefficient of drag, .29. Noise level, 58 dB at 60 mph.

The reaction from the army of engineers and technicians was unanimous: impossible! The goals were individually attainable but collectively unreachable. They all conflicted with one another. Greater speed needs more power. which means a heavier engine, which demands more fuel and makes more noise.

> Naokatsu. *Never compromise.*
> **Ichiro Suzuki**

Suzuki would accept nothing less than a V8 with a displacement of 4.0 liters. But trying to put a 4-Liter V8 into a lightweight luxury car was unheard of. Legend has it that product engineering chief Akira Takahashi told Suzuki he was crazy, but that Suzuki refused to leave Takahashi's office unless he agreed to attempt the engine at least once.

Months passed and progress slowed on all fronts. The look still wasn't right. Failures far outweighed successes. Designers and engineers were in conflict. Hundreds of prototypes would litter the trail. The project was taking its toll, and tensions were running high.

Suzuki pushed harder, moving the invisible lines in the org chart and creating working groups that cut across departments and divisions, with team leaders held accountable. Every problem was broken down to the smallest obstacle and tackled at its root. Design and engineering began to realize complementary goals. One by one, the elegant solutions appeared.

For example, aesthetics and aerodynamics complemented each other— fitting window glass and door handles into the metal itself yielded a cleaner look and better airflow. Sloping the rear window just enough to push air off the trunk and building a spoiler into the trunk lid to make the back end more stable resulted in a sleeker profile. The innovations kept coming.

The exterior was nearing the mark, but something was missing. Suzuki turned to Uchida, who called up Dezi to sketch a front end worthy of the world's best car. Dezi's sketch would be the keeper.

Late in the game, overall weight was still too high, fuel efficiency was off the mark, and the cabin wasn't quiet enough. Suzuki ordered an engine rebuild, invoking the spirit of the Zero, World War II's finest warplane and demanding the highest power, lowest weight, and finest precision. One could not be sacrificed for the other.

The solution was dramatic: an engine cast almost entirely from aluminum. Block, pistons, valve lifters, cam covers, everything. It works. The car is 120 pounds lighter than the BMW 735i, gets better mileage, and avoids the gas-guzzler tax.

Only the noise problem remained. A fuel-injected 4.0 liter V8 with double overhead camshafts and 32 valves with continuously variable valve timing packs a mean wallop. The goal was silence, or something very close to it: 58 decibels.

Every moving part was examined to find the noise. It was the shaft. Like most rear-wheel drive cars, the propeller shaft is in two parts, with an angled knuckle connecting them. The solution: Build a perfectly straight one. The noise disappeared.

By 1989 the car was ready. But the perfect car needed the perfect name, the perfect logo, the perfect tagline, and the perfect dealership. It could not be a Toyota. It wasn't a brand extension, it was a new brand. Lexus was chosen from hundreds of possibilities. In a departure from a typical product focused tagline, "The Relentless Pursuit of Perfection" appropriately defined the core philosophy. Only 81 of the very best dealers in the nation were selected out of 1600 possible candidates. Everything was in place.

When the Lexus LS400 went on sale September 1, 1989, it was by all objective measures the best in the world. Mission accomplished.

Now *that's* how to build a better mousetrap. So much better that upon tearing down two LS400s given to General Motors by a Southern California auto dealer, Cadillac engineers concluded that the Lexus cars could not be built. At least not by them.

The Lexus LS400 story gives a vivid portrayal of the innovation process behind an irrefutably elegant solution. Toyota redefined the luxury automobile by aggressively and ambitiously pursuing the highest

Formula for Perfection: How the Great Get Greater

Tiger Woods

In 1997, with barely seven months under his belt as a professional golfer, 20-year-old Tiger Woods stunned the golf world. It wasn't that he had won five PGA Tour tournaments. It wasn't that he had won the 1997 Masters by twelve strokes. It was his decision to reinvent his swing.

Pundits and peers thought he was crazy. But Tiger knew his swing wasn't as consistent, controlled, or efficient as it could be. Already a diligent professional known for poring over video footage of his performances, Woods cited the relentless drive for perfection behind Toyota's success. He explained how Toyota engineers will push the limits of the line until a breakdown occurs, fix it, then push it again. He spoke of *kaizen*, the Japanese word for "endless improvement and innovation."

It took eighteen months of rewiring, practice, and frustration, during which time he was virtually winless. Commentators speculated on his early demise. But Tiger knew he was getting better, and was quoted as saying, "Winning is not always the barometer of getting better." Slowly but surely, Tiger's new swing became a deadly controlled substance. With no loss of power, he could hit any type of shot on demand, better and more accurately than ever.

The payoff was a record six straight wins starting in late 1999. Since then, Tiger Woods has come to own the game. Yet he continues to perfect his swing.

Lance Armstrong

For seven-time Tour de France winner Lance Armstrong every second counts. The 2005 Tour Stage 4 saw Armstrong's Discovery Team win the time trial by a scant two seconds, the slimmest margin in Tour history.

After his first Tour victory in 1999, Armstrong nicknamed his legendary support team "F1," in deference to Formula One as the pinnacle of motorsport racing. He surrounded himself with equipment makers, clothing providers, and teammates who could help him shave even a fraction of a second off his performance, pushing them to do just that. Just a half second per kilometer saved Lance a 20-second advantage in a 40-kilometer time trial.

Armstrong spent hours in the wind tunnel, experimenting with every aspect, including infinitesimal shifts in his own body position, seeking the elusive perfect form. Annual progress was barely perceptible. But when he began his sweep in 1999, carbon fiber equipment, aerodynamic foil geometry, and dimpled clothing were reserved for rocket science. They are now standard gear not just for the elite cyclists, but for the recreational enthusiasts as well.

Little by little, Armstrong changed his game, and *the* game, forever—changing how cyclists approach their sport, how they prepare, how they perform, and how they compete. His innovative methods set new benchmarks across the board. And at the heart of his efforts was the relentless drive for perfection.

ideal possible. Obviously there exist many more facets to the story than can be told in a few short pages. But a host of immediate innovation imperatives abound.

Like how you have to time it right. How you need a clearly visible milestone. How you must thoroughly understand value through your customers' eyes. How nothing less than full commitment will work. How you need to break the problem down to its smallest definable elements and attack each one with ingenuity. How you must drive through the creative tension born of contradictory goals. How you have to match talent to task. How big leaps forward are achieved not in one big swag but through the cumulative effect of a multitude of much smaller hits. How innovation is not an event-driven thing, but a process. How significant departures from the brand require different identities, organizational structures, and distribution systems. How necessary it is to circumvent or manage competing corporate interests. How intelligent risk—defined as testing the limits of a proven capability—managed well, pays off handsomely. How you learn much more from failure than success. And how successful business innovation really *is* about finding a way to do something better than it's ever been done before.

You couldn't ask for a better primer on pursuing perfection.

SMALL AND STEADY

Take a lesson from the Lexus story. If you want big leaps, take small steps. If you want quantum impact, sweat the details. If you want to boil the ocean, do it one cup at a time. If you want excitement, get boring: Think method. Think metrics. Think micro.

Chasing perfection through relentless improvement builds the capability needed to achieve cross-company innovation. There's no downside to growing a strong portfolio of small

Perspective

Mass manufacturing perfection is no easy feat. Accommodating the demands of the handmade precision craftsmanship needed to produce the Lexus LS400 meant heavy investments in new tools and techniques. A new engine foundry was needed. Welds needed to be nearly twice as strong. Die casts needed to be twice as precise as those of Toyota cars. Fit and finish, the true acid test of luxury, needed to be virtually flawless.

In the end, Toyota spent upward of a billion dollars on building the LS400. But then, having thirty times that in cash on hand puts the resource risk in perspective.

ideas. Dealing in smaller currency lets you experiment more, get results quicker, and learn faster. Without fretting over risk. The more ideas you have, the more patterns and possibilities emerge. Which gives you more opportunities to combine and multiply ideas into bigger ones. The multiplier effect of compounding ideas is enormous. And when the big idea hits, which it will when the time is right, it'll be the daily incremental innovation you get from chasing perfection that will sustain your competitive advantage. And protect you from imitators. Your portfolio will remain secret sauce, because routine ground singles don't catch the eye of scholars, competitors, or the media like home runs do.

> *Trifles make perfection, and perfection is no trifle.*
> **Michelangelo**

Those who fail to constantly ideate and initiate are destined to be the eternal followers. That's okay for some, even many. But refuse to adapt, and the near future may include the auction block. Adaptation is all about evolution through incremental progress. And lest you think you'll run out of things to improve or an irrational fear of diminishing returns kicks in, rest easy. Because the world keeps changing.

There's no more logical way to consistently achieve breakthroughs than through a discipline of increments. And no better way to increase the odds of finding the elegant solution. If you remember nothing else, remember this: *Imperfection drives all innovation.*

REFLECTION

In what areas is your organization an industry benchmark?

What opportunities exist to optimize quality, cost, and speed?

What role does pursuing perfection play in your work?

How many improvement ideas do you have under way?

How have you changed the work in the last week?

CHAPTER 3

The Rhythm of Fit

There exists a silent pulse of perfect rhythm...which connects us to everything.
George Leonard

A Matter of Context

A great innovation offers a meaningful improvement in the lives of others. It serves the great needs of society. It opens up new opportunities for the world to change for the better, if only a little. The elegant solution fits a need in such a way that it evokes an immediate *of course!* It's the right thing, at the right time, in the right form, for the right people. It fits right in like it's always been there.

Now that may *seem* simple, but it's harder than it appears. Since 2000, the average number of patents granted annually by the U.S. Patent & Trademark Office is 182,585. Historical evidence shows that only about .2%, or 365—one a day—will go on to become useful innovations for society. That's the difference between invention and innovation.

Behind that number is the notion of *context*, aka conditions for success. Build a better mousetrap, and the whole world beats a path to your door *only* if the conditions are just right. First of all, you'd better be overrun with mice. Which means that the existing mousetrap isn't doing what it oughta, or, more likely, something else is going on that the current mousetrap maker didn't consider. Chances are it's not about the mousetrap. If you don't understand the failure intimately, your mousetrap won't do much better no matter how jiffy it is.

Enter the need to think beyond the obvious, to think through cause and effect, through the repercussions of our actions and decisions. Because it's the system governing the idea that provides the context. Seemingly great ideas get beaten by systems all the time.

The system rules.

WHEN SYSTEMS RULE

What separates inventors from innovators is the ability to think through all the conditions and connections required to allow a solution to fit seamlessly into the everyday beat of those who will use it. That kind of thinking is *systems thinking*. It's the ability to provide solutions within the current context, or providing a new one along with the solution.

Systems thinking isn't natural, intuitive, or easy. And nowhere in our formative years do we get schooled in systems thinking. But it can be learned.

Thomas Edison was a systems thinker. He had to be to turn his invention into an innovation. He knew his little invention wouldn't change the world on its own. He knew, because incandescent lighting had already been developed, on the other side of the Atlantic. He knew the gas lighting industry—*the existing system*—held the real power, and a lightbulb alone wasn't going to dethrone it. He knew the elegant solution was about providing on-demand light and power to everyone. And that required a whole new system to provide the proper context in which the lightbulb could flourish.

In under three years and mostly with his own money, Edison built the entire electric power system. He designed, engineered, and manufactured everything down to wiring: constructing power stations to convert steam power to electricity, digging and laying miles of wiring, insulating the wires to prevent damage and discharge due to moisture, and connecting the conduits in a workable network. He built and installed electric motors in the various types of machinery that would use the new power source, along with all the infrastructure needed to support the use of electricity, like meters, fuse boxes, lamp holders, switches, and sockets.

Sakichi Toyoda was a systems thinker. He understood the problem facing his mother and, in fact, all the other married women in his community. Although he lived in a rural farming community, every house had a loom, which enabled each wife to make extra income. He saw the problem in its full context, so his approach had the proper perspective. The problem was personal stress and strain. He didn't set out to build a better loom as much as to alleviate the human difficulties created by insufficient tools and methods. That was the great and pressing need. Framing the problem that way had everything to do with building a commercially successful loom.

> *Business and human endeavors are systems…we tend to focus on snapshots of isolated parts of the system, and wonder why our deepest problems never get solved.*
> **Peter Senge**

Both Edison and Toyoda realized success because everything fit. They made sure of it. But what happens when it doesn't? Fast-forward to 1956 when Toyota made its debut on American soil. The story of the Toyota Toyopet Crown makes the case.

In 1950, Shotaro Kamiya, then-president of the newly formed Toyota Motor Sales Company, Ltd. in Japan, took a trip to America. He noticed that there wasn't a single small car on the road. But on a return visit in 1955, things had begun to change.

Following World War II, Americans had begun to move out to the suburbs. The need for a second car was growing. But a second car of American make was unaffordable. This need, Kamiya realized, was igniting sales growth of inexpensive, foreign compact cars. The Volkswagen Beetle was very popular. Imports were highly visible in markets like Los Angeles. Numbers were approaching 100,000 units a year—still less than 1% of the market, but on the rise.

Kamiya discovered that the major American automakers showed little interest in the small-car market because of low profit margins and little demand. Based on the growth curve, Kamiya predicted that imports might own 10% of the market, or 700,000 cars in 1955. That number represented a decade's worth of production from all of Japan's car companies combined.

Kamiya seized the opportunity to begin exporting to the United States, reasoning that if growth continued, Detroit might seek protection from imports. If that happened before Toyota gained a foothold in America, the company might be permanently cut off from the world's largest auto market. He returned to Japan, and began to set the wheels in motion.

And Kamiya had the perfect car, the Toyopet Crown. The small sedan had become an overnight sensation in Japan when it made its debut in 1955. It was a huge hit with taxi drivers in Tokyo.

Research confirmed that the Los Angeles area would be an ideal base of operations. L.A. was the leading market for imported cars in the United States, and provided easy convenience as a port of entry.

On August 25, 1955, two Toyopet Crowns were loaded on a ship for the United States. "I will never forget the feeling I had when those first two sample cars sailed from Yokohama. It was like seeing my children off on a long journey."

The journey wouldn't be quite as long as he anticipated or hoped.

Unlike its debut in Japan, the Toyopet Crown was an overnight flop when it hit the streets of L.A. in the spring of 1956. Its design wasn't suited for the U.S. highway system. Driven at normal freeway speeds of 60 mph, it lost power, overheated, and shook violently. It consumed excessive gas and oil. The interior cabin was ill-suited for the average American, with their long legs and arms. Anyone over medium height had difficulty negotiating the limited headroom. The car failed miserably and was yanked from the market.

It would be another eight years before Toyota would try again, successfully, with a car built specifically for the American market.

By not properly framing the problem and seeing the proposed solution in the right context, by neglecting the system in which the idea must flourish, what appeared to be a great opportunity to serve a real social need became an embarrassing blunder. The little Toyopet Crown simply didn't fit in on the fast flowing L.A. freeways.

That glaring failure, and the ability to learn from it, became a driving force behind Toyota's newfound respect for systems. Toyota leaders at all levels vowed never again to design and market another product in a vacuum. They returned to their roots.

Thinking It Through

A casual perusal of daily news headlines drives home the stark realization that we're just not that good at the main systems thinking requirement of getting a decent bead on long-term cause and effect. Some stories bring a chuckle as they become fodder for the late-night comics.

In the spring of 2005 a news story reported that ivory poachers in Africa defeated themselves, permanently. The poachers couldn't understand why, after butchering male elephants for generations to harvest the tusks, there was no ivory left to poach. There were plenty of male African elephants, all right. Just non-tusked ones. The explanation rests in the system. By killing off all the tusked males and leaving only the non-tusked to survive, the no-tusk gene became dominant, while the gene for tusks gradually disappeared. No tusk, no ivory, no business.

In the early 1970s insects defeated the U.S. Army. The tiny three-mile long Micronesian island of Kwajalein, run by the army, was being overrun with flies. It was becoming more than a pesty situation for the 5,000 U.S. citizens living there. People had to keep moving just to keep the flies off. No one wanted to wear insect repellant 24/7. Someone in the Army Corps of Engineers discovered that a certain kind of wasp was the natural predator of flies. By importing a critical mass of wasps, so the thinking went, the flies and wasps would develop a balanced ecosystem. No such luck. The wasps found more attractive tropical prey, and left the flies alone. So the island now had double trouble: flies *and* wasps. Funny, if you're a fly or wasp.

United Airlines's $700 million high-tech automated baggage system became the butt of jokes as it delayed the opening of the Denver International Airport well over a year and then regularly chewed up or lost luggage. The system featured miles of underground track with cart-to-computer communication via radio frequencies, and promised to revolutionize the airport experience. Television crews covering the debut split their sides as they watched carts overshoot luggage onto the tracks and get sliced up by other carts. After a rather painful ten years and nearly a billion dollars in operating costs, United's chief operating officer was quoted as saying, *"We have come to the conclusion that going to a manual approach is best."*

But some stories aren't so funny.

August 2005 caught the city of New Orleans unprepared to withstand the fury of Hurricane Katrina, a gulf storm of biblical proportions that destroyed the city. The totality of the destruction might have been mitigated, even prevented. The threat of a devastating hurricane or massive flood striking New Orleans was well known—several books and articles had foretold the possible consequences. In fact, just such a disaster had occurred a half century earlier when the North Sea Flood of 1953 destroyed the Netherlands. The similarity of the two events was eerie. Both geographical locations were situated in a delta region below sea level. Both locations had long histories of weathering lesser storms. Both storms had conditions of extremely high tides and winds. In both instances, the storm had been accurately predicted by the weather service. Both places were protected by a deficient levee system that had been neglected due to redirected funds. Both times scientists and engineers had analyzed the worst-case scenario and warned of it. And most astonishingly, in both cases early warnings went unheeded.

Late in 2005, General Motors announced a massive layoff of 30,000 workers, accompanied by nine factory closings. Less than two weeks later, Ford nearly matched the cut by announcing their own layoff of 25,000 and even more plant shutdowns. Both manufacturers found themselves crumbling under the weight of a faulty system they had created over fifty years earlier in the boom years following World War II, when they committed to an already extravagant, union-governed wage and benefit scheme far beyond the foreseeable future. As the Detroit three steadily lost market share to the Asian and European imports beginning in the early 1980s, they failed

Zero-Sum Game

In 2003 Mitsubishi Motors, a going concern in the United States owing only to a multibillion-dollar bailout by Japan, attempted to turn around their dismal sales figures with a promotion called "Zero-Zero-Zero." Car buyers got a car with no money down, no payments, and no interest for one full year. As it turns out, the program was aptly named. Thousands scooped up the offer, drove the car for the year, then let the car get repossessed. Losses approached a half-billion dollars.

Not two years later, Detroit's Big Three headed down the same shortsighted path in the summer of 2005 with their combined "employee pricing" and deep-discount financing to clear a glut on lagging models.

In both cases, the ability to think well through cause and effect was disturbingly absent. And the fact that no one was buying the cars in the first place never quite registered. By the end of 2005, GM would face a total loss of more than $10 billion.

to address their labor and production systems, both ailing from underlying problems masked by three decades of success.

But why couldn't U.S. automakers see that they were painting themselves into a corner, creating an eventually unsustainable situation in which too many retirees would have to be supported by too few workers? Why didn't New Orleans learn from the Dutch devastation or act on clear caution from knowledgeable sources in an effort to *prevent* the likely occurrence of a similar disaster?

The answer is a fundamental inability to think through, and accept, the likely ripple effect of events too far away in space or time. In other words, poor *foresight*. That, and a failure to provide the proper context for appropriate action. In other words, poor *insight*. Unfortunately, the "we'll cross that bridge when we get to it" mindset is the enemy of systems thinking. We're never short on *hindsight*, though. And hindsight being what it is, the tendency is to blame systemic failures like these on organizational culture. It's a favorite target, but not the right one.

Culture is the catchall phrase for an amalgam of organizational values, beliefs, and norms. It rests upon, is shaped by, and draws its power from, underlying systems and structures. While it is most certainly a contributing source, it is not the root cause of the problem. Since culture is closer to the surface of the issues, explicit, and thus more readily observed, it naturally and understandably becomes the target of attention. But as Toyota Production System engineer Taiichi Ohno always counseled: *"Address 'root cause' rather than 'source.' Root cause lies hidden beyond the source."* That is to say, if you want to change the culture, start by examining the power base on which it rests.

Let's look closer.

Averting Disaster

Advance warning of a possible West Coast port labor lockout in 2002 sparked a rapid response at Dell Inc., who stood to lose millions if essential computer parts were held prisoner out at sea.

The plan included chartering 18 Boeing 747s at $500,000 per plane, enough cargo space to house parts for 180,000 PCs. Round-trip flights to Shanghai and Taipei were managed in 33 hours. Dell's logistics experts were on the ground in every major Asian harbor, ensuring that Dell's cargo was loaded last, in order to be first out in unloading when ports reopened.

When the strikes hit, Dell wasn't caught flat-footed. While supply chains around the world were paralyzed for 10 days, Dell continued its business as usual without delaying a single customer order. *That's* systems thinking.

Working the System

It Takes a Systems Thinker

Tokyo, 2005 – Prime Minister Junichiro Koizumi needed an elegant solution for the wicked problem he saw looming on Japan's horizon. The birthrate was shrinking and the population was aging—a fifth of the populace was over 60. That meant a workforce contraction was coming, which would significantly diminish future productivity, in turn limiting growth. The economy was better but still sluggish from the previous decade's stagnation following financial market implosion. Something had to be done to drag Japan into the twenty-first century.

Junichiro knew his country needed a socioeconomic innovation. And he knew what it was: privatization of Japan Post, the ancient and massive monolithic government-owned postal institution with nearly 25,000 offices, 400,000 civil servant employees, and three trillion dollars (330 trillion yen) in assets, including nearly two trillion in savings and insurance deposits. Which made it far more than just a post office.

Japan Post was in fact the largest bank on the planet.

Privatizing it would provide enormous socioeconomic benefit. It would jumpstart the economy by releasing the enormous funds to more effective investment. It would rechannel money earmarked for propping up Japan's dead or dying rural economies with wasteful and ill-fitting public works projects, toward investment in growing cities and successful industries. It would ensure savvy capital investment based on potential return, not political ties and business favoritism.

Junichiro had the solution in mind: restructure the whole system and split it into four separate private businesses—mail delivery, banking, insurance services, and managing employee salaries and post-office properties.

Just one thing stood in his way: Japan's political system. His own party had joined the opposition to defeat his bill in the lower house of parliament. The system had won round one. But Junichiro was a crafty systems thinker. He knew the enemies of change and progress in his house. In true aikido fashion, he used the power and policy of the parliamentary system to oust all 37 of the rebels from the party. He worked the system within the rules to hold snap elections to replace them, bringing in like-minded candidates far more attractive to the people. Former Olympic athletes. A hero tycoon or two. A celebrity chef. Even a former Miss Tokyo.

The result was a landslide win and a truly stunning victory. Japan Post would now go the way of dinosaurs. And Junichiro is just getting started with his systems reforms.

The Elusive Innovation Culture

Creating a climate conducive to everyday innovation hinges on the ability to build the kinds of systems and structures that produce the environmental context needed to drive desired outcomes. A few noteworthy examples make the point.

The *9/11 Commission Report* in 2004 cited the most important failures as being "lack of imagination" and "cultural asymmetry," explaining that "To us, Afghanistan seemed very far away. To members of al Qaeda, America seemed very close." No, a small, highly organized, well-funded, and extremely inventive organization successfully accomplished a goal because their systems and structures were properly focused to do so. And the U.S. intelligence systems and agency structures were simply no match, because they were designed primarily for enforcement and only secondarily for prevention. Just the reverse of the need.

Memories of the *Challenger* space shuttle disaster of 1986 were still clear in our minds when the *Columbia* exploded over Texas in 2003. The tragedy brought with it an onslaught of criticisms, most of which centered on the NASA *culture*. The report of the Columbia Accident Investigation Board blamed "broken safety culture," "can-do culture," and "perfect place culture" as being behind the neglect of early warning signs and clear equipment failures discounted as "in-family" events. No, NASA's key processes were inherently biased to operate on inputs designed to produce the desired output: *liftoff*. Not mission delay.

In these cases, systems designed for one thing were used for another. As Charles Perow notes in his book *Normal Accidents,* such ill-fitted systems will inevitably fail. And in each case, the remedies revolved around bolstering systems and structures, not culture.

In the case of 9/11, the Commission recommendations were to "routinize" and "put in place systems" and "provide a framework" for analyzing improbable scenarios. That sounds like systems thinking. They suggested having a "coordinating mechanism" to ensure intelligence goals are met. The cabinet-level Department of Homeland Security was formed. And that sounds like structure.

Likewise, in the case of NASA, when the near-miss of the 2005 *Discovery* mission reminded everyone of the agency's shortcomings, new administrative leadership promised to refocus the organization by resetting priorities and measures, realigning programs and processes, and restructuring.

Big Company Syndrome

It's no big secret why culture is the favorite culprit named for a lack of creativity and innovation. It pulls together all the most visible company dynamics: management styles, budget policies, political practices, office environment, interpersonal relationships, and decision speed. But there's a deeper root cause related to the system and structure from which the culture springs: *Big Company Syndrome*.

Prevalent in large corporations with weak or loosely defined systems and structures, it goes something like this: Constant, company-wide innovation is not something requested, managed, or measured at the organizational level. Therefore the desire for personal reward and recognition drives an informal system intended to produce a promotion and bonus, which results in a strong *program mentality*. That is, sell a program up and request more resources in the form of bodies and budget, regardless of whether it adds value. Approval is assured because it produces a favor owed and supports the boss's own career ambitions. Objectives now become focused on meeting budget projections. Company expenses then rise faster than sales, and add further complexity. That limits organizational effectiveness, requiring even more work to execute the program, leading to yet further requests for more resources. When costs swell, senior management puts the squeeze on to stem the tide. Speed bumps get erected, usually in the form of additional project approvals. Valuable ideas get iced along with circumspect programs. Eventually, the ability to flex, react, and innovate is lost. It's something many large companies struggle with.

Compare that to a design studio or entrepreneurial outfit, both of which organize themselves around customer-focused goals, projects, and processes, not functions. Projects have a clear start and stop, so resources are mobilized to match the need. But over a certain size, the entrepreneurial structure grows up and gives ground to the Big Company Syndrome.

Can the Big Company Syndrome be turned around? Is there a way to produce the creative shop experience and entrepreneurial spirit to ensure constant innovation even when the Big Company Syndrome has a stranglehold on the organization? Yes, through strong systems and solid structures focused on creating the right social context. A number of companies have done this, but perhaps none better than Toyota. The story of the joint partnership between Toyota and General Motors in the mid-1980s tells the story.

NUMMI

Many have speculated that much of Toyota's success can be attributed to "Japanese management" or the so-called "Japanese business culture." A more accurate assessment would attribute much of their success to the systems they employ. Witness the miraculous transformation by Toyota of a General Motors factory in Fremont, California. It is an oft-told story, but one worth retelling in the context of understanding the power of systems and structures to produce a 360° innovation.

It was 1982, the first full year of Reaganomics, and trade friction was developing between the United States and Japan over the volume of import cars. American industry wasn't exactly booming. The General Motors (GM) plant in Fremont, California, was in a death spiral. It was GM's worst plant by far in terms of quality and productivity: double-digit defects in every car, with average hours to assemble a vehicle far higher than in any other GM plant. Lack of employee pride and confidence was evidenced by the absence of Fremont-built cars in the employee parking lot.

Labor conditions were militant, toxic, even violent, with multiple strikes and sickouts by the United Auto Workers. The plant had a backlog of some 5000 union grievances. Absenteeism topped 20%, requiring the hiring of that many more workers on any given shift. Rampant drug and alcohol abuse required special cleaning crews to clear the liquor bottles and drug paraphernalia from the employee lot after shift change.

Systems Failure
Of Greenfields and Support Systems

Most of the world recognizes the value of fuel cell technology to power automobiles in the future. Fuel cells produce energy from hydrogen and a chemical reaction that produces electricity. The only emission is water. The technology has been available for over a decade, and almost every carmaker has a test vehicle under development. The reason fuel cell cars aren't in showrooms isn't technology, it's the systems governing the technology. The investment in hydrocarbon infrastructure is so gigantic and the inertia so massive that it may take years, if not decades, for fuel cell cars to become a reality, at least in most developed countries.

One interesting exception is China. Many think China will win the fuel cell race. China doesn't have a huge fueling system in place. They alone have the greenfield opportunity and capacity to move quickly to a hydrogen system. As of this writing, car sales are exploding in China. That makes China the front-runner for leapfrogging straight into the future, much as most of the world moved quickly to wireless cellular telephones and left the hardwired system behind.

The cell phone is perhaps the most significant innovation since wheels, wallets, and watches. Everyone has one. Researchers forecast a billion units sold each year before 2010. It's changed the way we think and act. Yet cell phones don't work nearly as well as they could. It's not entirely a problem of handset technology. At the root of it all are systems issues raised by the telecom carriers owning the cellular networks.

Handset makers have to get approval from the network operators, who say they need to control the phones that run on their system to ensure service quality and safety. AT&T used the same line in the 1970s to justify their stranglehold on the industry. Customers couldn't buy the phone they wanted. They had to rent one from Ma Bell. We know how that turned out.

The battle of the systems will be fun to watch. Already the wireless broadband war is heating up as towns and cities take on the network providers to better serve their constituency by operating their own systems.

If you're wondering who will win, the smart money will be on the best systems thinker, and consumers.

In February, the factory closed, the entire workforce laid off.

Enter Toyota, looking to ease trade tensions and test its production system and management approach on U.S. soil with American unions and suppliers. GM's dark plant was the target. Toyota and GM formed a joint partnership in 1983 to reopen the Fremont line, naming it New United Motor Manufacturing Inc. (NUMMI). A rebadged Toyota Corolla and Chevrolet Prizm were to be the products.

The venture carried risk. Conditions of the deal posed seemingly insurmountable challenges. Toyota would inject cash, manage the plant, and implement the Toyota Production System. But there was a hiccup. They had to use the same workers, the same union, the same facilities and equipment. GM wanted the secrets of lean production and successful compact car design, and the UAW wanted recognition and representation.

Toyota itself was split, the primary concern being giving away production methods and quality processes to a direct competitor. Toyota Chairman Eiji Toyoda, though, saw it as the perfect challenge, the perfect experiment, and the perfect opportunity to test the viability and transportability of the Toyota Production System. It was the chance to see whether people of different cultures with different philosophies and attitudes could adapt to the Toyota system and structure. It was the necessary first step leading to wholly-owned Toyota manufacturing in North America.

Toyota took the highest road possible. They hired back 85% of the Fremont hourly union workforce. Workers would have a strong voice in plant operations. A no-layoff policy was instituted.

Nineteen eighty-four was spent ramping up operations. Toyota provided a new social context for work. They spent over $3 million to send 450 new group and team leaders to Toyota City for training in the Toyota Production System. UAW's hundred-plus line job descriptions were replaced by one: team member. Management hierarchy was flattened from fourteen levels to three: plant management, group leader, team leader.

Employees began participating in decisions regarding their work. Team

Elegant Solutions Save the Third World
Serving Those in Need Sparks Fitting Innovation

Michel Lescanne and Andre Briend are the systems thinkers behind Nutriset, a small French firm founded amid the great hunger crises of the 1980s. For nearly a generation, they have been fixated on solving the intractable problem of starvation in famine-ridden regions of Africa. Their pursuit centers on the idea of a universal nutritional antidote to malnutrition among children in the danger zones of Sudan, Congo, and Ethiopia. Dissatisfied with the conventional solutions of powdered-milk-based liquid mixes, the pair engineered their innovation by reframing the problem. The existing system relied on emergency feeding centers and medical professionals trained to mix powdered supplements with clean water, a rare commodity. Crowded clinical settings fostered disease, and required mothers to be present, which meant leaving their other hungry children behind in the village while they traveled. Emergency centers and milk mixes didn't address the real need: widespread routine managed care among the communities where hungry children live. Their idea: Plumpy'nut, a peanut goo combining taste and texture of European favorite Nutella spread, advanced nutrition, and the foil packet pouches now standard practice among athletes. The solution couldn't be more elegant. Plumpy'nut is self-contained, versatile, and inexpensive (35¢/packet); peanuts are a staple in Africa; no allergies exist; children love the taste; travel to centers is eliminated, along with the need for expert mixing with water. And three packets a day for a few weeks solves starvation—recovery rates in hunger hotspots have soared from 25% to 95%.

It doesn't take much to launch a startup in rural east Africa. In fact, $100 will do it. For nearly two decades, Silicon Valley nonprofit venture firm Valley Enterprise Fund has launched an average of 500 microbusinesses a year in remote regions including Uganda, Kenya, and Tanzania. In 1987, founder Brian Lehnen set out to solve the wicked problem of poverty in Africa. As he saw it, the issue wasn't one of charitable contribution. It was one of dignity. To achieve the greatest long-term impact on the lives of the poor, you had to tap the human potential and enable people to become self-sufficient, productive. Enable them to change their lives. His idea was microgrants: $50 of seed capital to start a business. If business goals are met within six months, another $50 grant is awarded. $50 has been all that's needed to start vegetable stands, dairy farms, bakeries, chicken farms, and bike parts stands. The results have been astounding. Many of the entrepreneurs expand and start second and third businesses. Valley Enterprise Fund figures every $100 helps to improve the lives of twenty-five people.

members were trained in problem solving and kaizen practices to become the experts in their respective operations. Employee roles expanded, the primary responsibility becoming one of proactive thinking and improving, not simply doing. Team leaders and members began engaging in group problem solving. Ideas for improvement were quickly implemented by team members, with successful solutions becoming standardized. All associates were empowered to stop the line at any time to fix a problem by pulling a cord running around the entire facility. Cooperation and confidence replaced coercion and conflict.

Full production began in 1985, and by year-end 1986, NUMMI had the highest quality and productivity of any GM plant. Quality defects dropped from 12 to 1 per vehicle. Cars were assembled in half the time. Absenteeism dropped to 3%. Worker satisfaction and engagement soared. Operational innovation was on the rise, with employee participation over 90% and nearly 10,000 ideas implemented. Same people, same union, same equipment. Radically different outcome. All in under two years.

By 1988, NUMMI was an award-winning plant. By 1990, the Toyota Production System was being heralded as the world-class standard for manufacturing operations.

Take-home lesson: change the context, change the system, and change the structure. Make it meaningful, and make sure everything fits.

Then watch the culture of innovation flourish.

> *The workings of a pin affect the workings of the entire nation.*
> **Kiichiro Toyoda**

DIMENSIONS OF FIT

Every solution is connected to a larger system. So searching for *elegant* solutions necessitates good systems thinking. That means understanding all the dimensions impacting cause and effect. And every solution has three governing dimensions.

- *Solid structure*—policies, procedures, physical environment.
- *Strong systems*—input, output, processes, patterns.
- *Social significance*—purpose, principles, people.

These elements give meaning to an innovation by providing the lens of context through which the solution can be viewed. People crave meaning, because it helps them make sense of the world.

Great innovation looks deep into each dimension. Thinking well through each facet builds the radar screen needed to tackle all the complexities, steps, and interactions required to ensure a good fit with society.

Now that sounds more atmospheric than it is. Words like *structure, systems,* and *significance* shouldn't frighten anyone. Systems thinking isn't about IQ. Just the opposite. It's about delivering something intuitive. It's about being street smart.

We need look no further for an everyday example of all three dimensions in action than the uniquely American innovation of the *franchise*. A franchise is a simple turnkey system. It's a standard-structure, small-scale, self-contained, transportable, repeatable, user-friendly system housing a central idea that fulfills a basic need in society.

Yes, the franchise concept is absolutely an elegant solution. And we have a true systems thinker to thank: traveling salesman-turned-burger emperor Ray Kroc, of McDonald's fame.

FINAL WORDS ON FIT

The stories and perspectives in this chapter highlight the critically important role *fit* plays in innovation. Great innovation is great in large part because of context. Context helps explain why some ideas take off and others don't. It's what separates invention from innovation. And context is shaped and governed by the prevailing systems and structures surrounding your ideas. So you have to pay attention to it.

Context is like the frame in art. If the canvas doesn't fit the frame, the whole thing doesn't quite work. The trouble is, we're often so concerned with the masterpiece inside that we forget the significance of the frame.

We're constantly being told to *think outside the box.* It's become an impotent platitude. Which is okay, because it's well off the mark. Most people in big outfits probably don't even have a clue what the box is. So you can't think outside it even if you wanted to.

The box is *context.* And you have two choices: make your idea fit inside the box, or build a brand new box to replace the old one. Some people call that disruptive, or destructive. Of course it is. So what? Creation *is* destruction. *New replacing old* is the way of the world. And if you don't deliver a new box for an idea that doesn't fit in the old box, you've got nothing to put your great idea in. So it'll float untethered in the ether as just another invention without application, until it gets anchored to context.

The most important thing in art is the frame. For paint, literally. For other arts, figuratively, because, without this humble appliance, you can't know where the art stops and the real world begins.
Frank Zappa

Great innovation seeks to find and fit the rhythm of change happening around us. At the same time it aims to lead that change by finding a way to do something better than it's ever been done before. Great innovation *is* a brand of leadership. Elegant solutions meld with society.

They help move the world.

REFLECTION

What systems surround and govern your solution or business?

How well does your solution fit into and work with those systems?

What new structures are required to make your solution fly?

What are the great and pressing needs your solution serves?

What reactions and vulnerabilities will your solution encounter?

PRINCIPLES INTO PRACTICES

Part One discussed at length the three principles that guide innovative energy toward elegant solutions: *ingenuity in craft, pursuit of perfection,* and *fit with society.*

At Toyota, they're absolute priority. They're the *reason why*—the must-dos and must-haves. They're all that's worth fighting for. Without them...well, business then becomes all about the money. And that's a balloon that will eventually burst. Sneak a peek at Toyota's competition in Detroit for proof.

But now comes the hard part—making these three principles actionable—bringing them to life, applying them to your world, and building a capability around finding elegant solutions. And that requires more ground-level concepts. *Practices.* The *how.*

But embedded and present in each of the ten key practices to be covered in Part Two are the three underlying principles of innovation.

> The real stumbling block to innovation in large organizations is not lack of creativity. It is unsureness about priorities.
> **Lewis Lehr**

part

2

practices
tools for the trip

CHAPTER 4

Let Learning Lead

Learning will always remain something of an art, but even the best artists can improve their technique.
David Garvin

Learning and Innovation Go Hand in Hand, but Learning Comes First

Problem: *Learning disabilities hinder 360° innovation.* The truth is, before anyone can innovate anything, learning must take place. Learning is how we convert ideas into action. It's the only process by which we improve and advance. So we either have to get it right, or rely on others who do. And that's not a position of strength.

Cause: *Learning is misunderstood and undervalued.* Real learning is not about books or lectures or workshops. It's not a special activity separate from work. We shouldn't stop work to start learning. Learning is an acquired capability, and a teachable discipline. It requires developing a strong skill and utilizing a sound process.

Solution: *Make learning the job.* Integrate it into the daily work as the one true way to innovate. Employ solid routines to solve problems, develop ideas and generate useful new knowledge. Accelerate the application of that new knowledge. Pilot everything first, and assume you won't get it right the first time. That way there's no failure, just deeper experience. You can't separate learning from innovation, but you can speed it up. Learning triggers creativity down the line. Learning makes the other nine practices work. It pulls them all together. So learning comes first.

That's called *learnership*.

LEARNERSHIP AND THE OHNO CIRCLE

It has been said that Toyota is the ultimate learning organization. What's interesting is that learning is so much a part of the air they breathe that most Toyota associates are likely to look at you funny if you ask them to describe their approach to learning. Sure, they have the explicit mechanisms like a corporate university, technical training centers, and knowledge management systems. Most big firms do.

But that's not it. There's something much more subtle, much more tacit. Mastery—*perpetual learning*—is so ingrained in the organization that it's been declared by many to be part of the Toyota DNA. And what makes learning at Toyota so different is that the concept revolves around pursuing the right questions rather than securing the right answers. What drives learning at Toyota isn't a need to know. It's a need to inquire. To *understand.* That's a fundamental departure from how most define learning. Toyota doesn't confuse training with learning. And the most fascinating thing is that humility is at the base of it all. Toyota most respects wisdom and insight. They're in awe of it.

> *Toyota achieves competitive advantage on the basis of its ability to learn more quickly and more consistently than competitors.*
> **Steven Spear**

What they teach isn't a hard skill. It's the softest skill known: *thinking*. How to think critically is something handed down from mentor to disciple. It's something so difficult to make explicit that you might question the intelligence of doing it here. But it's worth a shot, because learnership truly represents the keys to the kingdom.

Perhaps the best way to convey the subtlety of the many facets of learning at Toyota is through the story of the infamous Ohno Circle, so named after one of the engineering pioneers of the Toyota Production System, Taiichi Ohno. Many people have heard the legend and misunderstand the lesson to be about the power of observation. With any hope, you will come to understand that the message runs much deeper.

The story is best told through the words of someone who knew the man. In a message to the World Class Manufacturing Forum in May, 2002, Toyota senior managing director Teriyuki Minoura spoke of his experience with Mr. Ohno and the Ohno Circle.

"When I reflect on what Mr. Ohno taught us, one thing that stands out to me is that he taught us how to think. He taught us to think deeply. When I think about this, I think that perhaps the 'T' in TPS should stand not only for Toyota, but also for 'Thinking.' The 'Thinking Production System.'

Now I would like to relate a story of Mr. Ohno's teaching on thinking. Mr. Ohno often would draw a circle on the floor in the middle of a bottleneck area, and he would make us stand in that circle all day long and watch the process. He wanted us to watch and ask 'why?' over and over. You may have heard about the five 'whys' in TPS. Mr. Ohno felt that if we stood in that circle, watching and asking 'why?' better ideas would come to us. He realized that new thoughts and new technologies do not come out of the blue, they come from a true understanding of the process.

In my case, I thought it was strange when he asked me to go into the circle. But what could I say? I was a freshman and he was the big boss and a member of the board of directors! So I went into the circle and began to watch the process. During the first hour, I began to understand the process. After two hours, I began to see the problems. After the third and fourth hours, I was starting to ask 'why?' Finally, I found the root cause and started to think about countermeasures.

With the countermeasures in place, I reported back to Mr. Ohno what I had observed and the problems I saw and the countermeasures I put in place as well as the reasons for the countermeasures. Mr. Ohno would just say, 'Is that so?' and nothing more. He never gave us answers. Most of the time he wouldn't even tell us if what we did was good or bad.

Now I realize what Mr. Ohno was trying to do. He was trying to make us think deeply—and think for ourselves."

The story reminds us of the old Chinese proverb: *What I hear, I forget. What I see, I remember. What I do, I understand.*

LEARNERSHIP DECODED: THE SCIENTIFIC METHOD

Our most powerful learning experiences generally occur in a four-phase cycle of *(1) Questioning; (2) Solving; (3) Experimenting; (4) Reflecting.*

That's pretty intuitive. Everything starts with a question, which triggers an investigation and information-gathering effort. *How can I do that better?* That leads to the definition of a problem to be analyzed and solved. The search for possible answers to your question entails generating ideas, solutions, and corrective measures. By experimenting with one or more of the solutions, the most appropriate and effective is discovered. You then reflect on your experiments, observing your own thinking and actions. *How well did that work?* This in turn stimulates further questions, commencing the learning cycle again.

That basic cycle is formally known as *The Scientific Method.* It's been codified in various ways and applied in settings ranging from art to science to business to warfare.

Statistician Walter Shewhart first applied it in a nonscientific way, calling it Plan-Do-Study-Act, or **PDSA**. His student, Dr. W. Edwards Deming, taught it to the Japanese during the postwar U.S. military occupation in 1950, calling it *The Shewhart Cycle.* The Japanese changed the terminology slightly to Plan-Do-Check-Act, or **PDCA**, calling it *The Deming Wheel.*

The late Capt. John Boyd, a U.S. Air Force fighter pilot and an avid student of Toyota's processes, adapted the learning cycle to dogfights, terming it **OODA**: Observe-Orient-Decide-Act. He who operates within his opponent's OODA cycle, or turns through the four stages faster relative to the competitor, wins the fight.

The Department of Defense applies the cycle in its **Spiral Development** process of designing new battlefield technologies. And finally, paramilitary organizations such as police forces use Scan-Analyze-Respond-Assess, or **SARA**, as their central problem-solving model.

While Toyota officially recognizes only PDCA, they actually use all of these to some degree. Let's look closer at the process.

Power of Process

One reason so many people find it hard to be creative and so many companies find it hard to innovate is that they lack a consistent approach to the problems they face. And everything is a problem. Call it a challenge, call it an opportunity, call it whatever you wish, but the fact is that any time a gap exists between where you are and where you want to be, it's a problem that needs to be solved. A problem isn't a bad thing, and dropping the negative baggage around the term itself helps tremendously in the effort to replace fix-it thinking with more expansive, innovative thinking.

At the heart of all remarkable innovations in any realm lies a rigorous routine, a disciplined methodology. And the learning cycle is at the core of that process. By codifying it, applying it, teaching it and adopting it as your official *modus operandi*, you gain enormous benefits.

> A goal without a method is cruel.
> **W. Edwards Deming**

First, a common approach leads to common terminology. That terminology, if matched well to the task and goal, begins to build a common language. And language is so very important to creating the systems and structures that drive success.

Second, a common method focuses thought and action. It unifies them into a straight line that's easy for people to understand and follow. That's important, because everyone wants a road map, especially for more challenging ventures.

Finally, a common technique lends itself well to the use of supporting tools that help enhance the process. And tools often shape behavior.

Insist on a common approach, and it won't be long before you'll have an idea management system under development. And that's the key to improving your idea quotient—ideas per capita.

If you currently use a common method consistently—meaning *every time* and for *every idea*—congratulations. You're a rare breed, like Toyota. So keep at it. You know the power of the process. If you don't, read on, because there's a simple tool that can help.

Toward a Grand Unified Process

If you don't have a solid routine for solving problems, what should you do? What options exist and which might best fit your situation?

PDCA is the Toyota standard for a studied approach to shop floor problem solving and continuous improvement, but it's over a half-century

Spotlight on Spiral Development

The Spiral Development Process now becoming more prevalent with the U.S. Department of Defense is shaving years off the old evolutionary strategy of designing and developing weaponry. Under that approach, the goal was to build a complete system, then improve it in stages. The first would be built to about an 80% solution. The second to 90% and the third to 100%. The problem being that it was taking too long getting new technology into the field. And when you're in the throes of fighting a war, the soldier on the battlefield needs the latest and greatest, quickly. Using the evolutionary approach it might take a decade or more to deliver a complex fleet of aircraft or a weapons system, effectively rendering it obsolete on arrival.

The Spiral Development Process represents a fast cycle learning method amounting to "build a little, test a little, build a little," its rapid, iterative process providing the opportunity for users, testers, and developers to interact. In an April 12, 2002 memo to the Chairman of the Joint Chiefs of Staff, Under Secretary of Defense E. S. Aldridge Jr. states, *"In this process, the require-ments are refined through experimentation and risk management, there is continuous feedback, and the user is provided the best possible capability..."*

Here's how it works. A DOD program office identifies a desired capability but does not specify how the final system is to be built. A given system is broken down into its component systems and designed in a modular fashion, enabling individual parts to develop before being integrated into a single system. So a problem with one component won't necessarily slow development of others. After the first production release is delivered, the contractor tests new features and technologies, consulting with the program office on which ones are ready for use. Spiral Development solves the challenge of how to keep a platform current while it's being built.

For example, the recent restructuring of the army's $100 billion Future Combat System, which features eighteen separate cutting edge components, including a wireless network enabling better field communications, robots, and unmanned vehicles. Under the evolutionary approach, all components would have been developed before fielding. The new plan is to get parts of the system out to the battlefield by 2008, and spiral in the rest.

old and may be limited for dynamic open-ended systems innovation. The terms don't quite capture the creativity.

SARA has its roots in community policing, and has usefulness in investigatory and quick-response situations. Toyota uses a similar approach in resolving customer relations issues.

OODA cycles focus on the competitor, rather than a product or service. It's more of a relative learning cycle. Toyota's competitive strategy takes on this brand of learning in launching new products and technologies, and in marketing and sales.

SPIRAL Development is best for complex system development and rapid prototyping. Toyota uses a form of this methodology throughout its product design and engineering process.

There is another, more universal option. Take the best parts from all the various versions of the learning cycle, distill them down into terms that make sense for innovation, and you have a method that looks and sounds like this:

Investigate

Design

Execute

Adjust

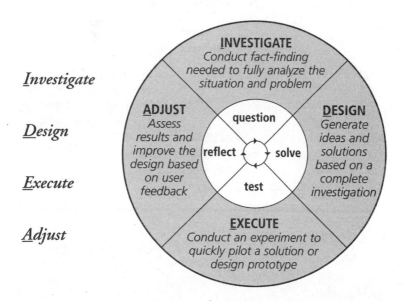

I.D.E.A. Loops! Fast or slow, short or long, IDEA Loops capture the central cycle behind real-world innovation in an intuitive way.

ToolKit: IDEA Loops

A physician in the emergency room. A criminalist at the scene of the crime. An inventor in his workshop. An artist at her easel. A scientist in the laboratory. An operator on a 911 call. A factory associate on the shop floor. A copywriter crafting a new advertisement. An engineer programming new software.

What they all have in common is IDEA Loops. They all perform the same basic activities. It's just the subject matter that varies. The time frame they work under varies. How they do it varies. The environment in which they do it varies.

The beauty of IDEA Loops is that they can apply to all situations. Investigation, Design, Execution, and Adjustment are the universal common denominators to successful innovation. Still, a little definition is in order. Each phase is focused on a few key questions.

Investigate
What are you trying to do and why?
What are the facts and issues?
What's the problem and cause?

Adjust
What worked, what didn't, and why?
What adjustments must be made?
What are the next steps?

Design
What does perfection look like?
What ideas exist for achieving it?
What is the best solution?

Execute
What do you expect will happen?
How will you test the solution?
What is the scope of impact?

A simple tool accompanies IDEA Loops: The IDEA Brief.

ToolKit: IDEA Brief

The IDEA Brief is a simple one-page report that captures the essence of the idea and leads the reader through the thinking. A template and example follow.

Purpose:	**Author:**
What are you trying to do, and why?	**Date:**

INVESTIGATE

Current State:

Facts, issues, intelligence, symptoms, relevant observations, and data—the goal is to describe, define, and grasp the present depth and breadth of the current "as is" situation, using graphics and visual presentation if possible.

Problem:

Succinct statement that properly frames the problem, gap, challenge, or opportunity as you see it, based on the current reality.

Cause:

Diagnosis of the problem, challenge, or opportunity: Why does it exist?

DESIGN

Future State:

Picture of the ideal as it relates to the theme and outcome of investigation—what does perfection look like?

Best Solution:

The short list of ideas, solutions, options, and countermeasures to achieve the future state; high-level description of the best solution.

EXECUTE

Key Goals:

Specific success indicators: Goals, objectives, measures—expected outcomes.

Implementation:

Overview of key steps in a rapid pilot plan.

Expected Impact:

Effect on the system, structure, and stakeholders; measurable benefit to customers.

ADJUST

Reflection:

Feedback on what worked, what didn't, and why or why not; implications and recommendations for the future; new insights gained; new questions to consider and pursue.

| Purpose: Create a painless credit approval proposal for business banking clients. | Author: W. F. Banks |
| | Date: 10-15-06 |

INVESTIGATE

Current State:
Complex loan process for business clients is lengthy and difficult.
Multiple reviews are required by senior bankers, requiring multiple corrections/rewrites.
Approximately 10,000 business loans processed annually.
Average completion/cycle time per loan is 32 hours; average number of errors requiring return to banker is 6; turnaround time to client is 21 days.
Average internal cost per loan is $4400; $44 million/year

Problem:
Inexperienced bankers have great difficulty completing credit approval proposals, resulting in enormous delays, error correction, redundancy, and lost opportunity cost.

Cause:
Current process does not distinguish between complex and simplex financial analysis.

DESIGN

Future State:
One-pass credit approval process—no errors, no rework
One-week approval

Best Solution:
Create a standard cut-and-paste template online for facilitating credit analysis and review process, enabling banker to answer questions to proper specification and complete credit approval proposal accurately and thoroughly.

EXECUTE

Key Goals:
Complete cycle time of 9 hours (vs. current 17); 0 returns/rework
7-day client turnaround (vs. current 21)

Implementation:
1. Develop template; 2. Educate bankers; 3. Test for one month; 4. Track metrics

Expected Impact:
Reduced burden on all bankers; improved client satisfaction
Blended savings (productivity plus cost) = $2380/loan; $23.8 million/year savings

ADJUST

Reflection:
Actual time reduction of 33% (21 to 14 days) vs. planned 67% (21 to 7 days).
Template deemed desirable; 86% of bankers will use the template on a regular basis.
Recent system redesign requires template revision.
To test the effectiveness of the new template format, a second pilot will be run.

LEARNERSHIP & HANSEI

Hansei (hahn-say) is the Japanese word for reflection. Hansei is the rigorous review conducted after action has been taken. It's a huge and absolutely vital part of learning. And with a few notable exceptions, our Western culture is just plain miserable at it.

Hansei is not about confirmation. It's not about celebration of success. It's a sobering reality check, regardless of a project's outcome. Were you to attend a hansei meeting following a resounding success at Toyota, you would be shocked at the tone of the meeting. It's stern and serious. Fine, the team greatly exceeded expectations. Guess what, that means they didn't understand their process. Their objectives should have been met. And even if they matched perfectly to the target, the team must still examine the course of action and the interim measures, not just the final results.

In Western culture, about the only time anything close to true hansei occurs is when a catastrophic failure happens. *9/11. Columbia. Hurricane Katrina.* Even then, it's a "special study," generally focused more on conducting a fault-finding autopsy in order to place blame more than anything else. When projects meet their objective, we celebrate. Unfortunately, there's little in the way of deep learning in that approach. Our Western cultural bias for action doesn't value reflection nearly as highly as it should. Horrors, if we catch anyone in their office staring out into space, they must be daydreaming, goofing off.

We just don't seem to get it. It's about *thinking*. Hansei fosters real learning and insight. Our shortcomings in this area have everything to do with why so many individuals and organizations suffer from self-induced learning disability in business.

Hansei is indeed an Eastern cultural artifact. Its true meaning is closer to *introspection* than *reflection*. Hansei finds its roots in religion, but it is a profound skill to be mastered. Japanese schoolchildren are taught from kindergarten how to perform hansei, and it is a significant tool used to improve one's self. The key insight is this: *Hansei is performed regularly, irrespective of performance!* Hansei flies in the face of the *if it ain't broke don't fix it* mindset. Fortunately, we can learn to build hansei into our efforts to solve problems innovatively. And there's a specific tool that will help.

The Art & Science of Reflection

Without thinking, there will be no innovation, no elegant solution. And behind every innovative thought is a trail of reflection. Reflection is an important part of invoking ingenuity, at both the individual and organizational level. Done right—*right for the thinker*—the outcome is very nearly always better perspective and insight. Just ask Bill Gates.

Bill Gates's "Think Week"

Now legendary Think Week is the solitary sabbatical taken twice yearly by Microsoft founder and chairman Bill Gates. In his tiny lakeside cottage hideaway, Bill Gates ponders the past, present, and future of his company, of technology, and of his industry. He reads 100 or more white papers submitted by employees, responding to each one by making handwritten comments in the margins. He takes long walks along the lake shore in contemplation. He leverages the ideas of others to spark those of his own. He analyzes his own performance. He analyzes disappointments. He analyzes the wins. He reflects. He introspects.

He performs hansei.

Exercise: Personal Hansei

Even if five minutes is all you can spare, set aside time each day for personal hansei—reflecting and introspecting. Tailor the approach to find what works best for you.

Here's what to do:

1. Designate a time and place devoted to daily solitude.

2. Use this time to reflect on your work, your activities, your plans.

3. Rigorously critique both successes and failures of the day.

4. Look for connections among seemingly unconnected things.

5. Develop questions, new ideas, and "what if" hypotheses.

6. Identify opportunities to try out new ideas.

ToolKit: After Action Reviews

The practical application of hansei is the After Action Review (AAR), developed by the U.S. Army. AARs are such a part of the army methodology that the term has become a verb. *"We AARed it."*

In a nutshell, an AAR is a regular meeting held after every key milestone. The word *regular* is important. AARs aren't special studies. They're not just conducted at the conclusion of an action. The regularity builds the learning discipline. The AAR is a standard operating procedure.

> *The Army's After Action Review (AAR) is arguably one of the most successful organizational learning methods yet devised.*
> **Peter Senge**

An AAR is simple in concept. The meeting has an explicit goal of learning, with a clear objective of answering three basic questions: *1. What was supposed to happen? 2. What actually happened? 3. Why were there differences?*

The tool's power lies in its simplicity. The three questions allow the learning needed for future improvement. But learning doesn't occur without open communication in a transparent environment where it's safe to tell the absolute truth. So there are some rules.

Attendance by all involved is mandatory—no show, no AAR. No outside facilitation. No fault-finding or blaming—focus on tasks and goals only. Specific AAR facts are confidential and to be used for analysis, learning, and improvement only—no personnel actions arising from AARs allowed.

Organizations that have successfully internalized AARs have learned to learn. BP, GE, and Motorola are just a few. Learning hospitals use a form of AARs to effectively conduct a post-surgery morbidity conference.

By the way, you've already had a taste of hansei if you've been diligent in considering the questions at the end of each chapter. From here on, we'll use the word *hansei*. It's more accurate.

This Is Only a Test

Without a solid learning routine, we can't get a good handle on the intricacies of cause and effect. But there's good news.

Time to Learn

Toyota factory associates conducting experiments will come in early before their shift to perform dry runs, often using cardboard and other makeshift materials to mock up prototypes of tools and equipment. Working through shift changes and staying late to make adjustments and create new standards is common.

First, learning cycles come naturally. But they got replaced by institutional education as we grew up. So all we really have to do is get back in touch with them and *practice*. And learning cycles aren't complicated. They're all around us. So much so that we often discount them. The next time you see an infant in a high chair throwing food on the floor, know that you're watching a learning cycle in action. She's wondering what will happen if she drops her strained carrots. The problem is how to get them on the ground. She could tip her dish over the tray, flick her spoon, or grab a fistful and toss away. She tries the tip. It works. Great feedback from the dish as it crashes on the tile. She confirms her test by doing it again after mom picks it up. It works so well she adopts it as her current preferred method. Lesson learned, though: Mom doesn't like it. So she launches another experiment.

Second, and perhaps most critically important to realize, there is no failure in the learning cycle. If you've ever wondered why pilot projects never fail while big, change-the-world projects almost always do, it's because the goal of any pilot is to learn. So you can't help but succeed. It's the difference between movies and TV. TV producers always pilot a new series with a few episodes to see the audience response. Movie producers develop the final product with a bet-it-all gambit, relying on past experience as the key input. That's risky, very risky.

Learnership is all about the *beta*. IDEA Loops help drive a fast learning cycle of testing, experimenting, piloting, and prototyping.

Hansei

How is new insight systematically captured in your organization?

To what degree is experimentation built into core work processes?

What processes are in place to quickly pilot new ideas?

How does your organization view and handle failure?

How quickly does your team act on new information and ideas?

CHAPTER 5

Learn to See

Fortune favors the prepared mind.
Louis Pasteur

Elegant Solutions Often Come from Customers—Get Out More and Live in Their World

Problem: *Solutions don't work as imagined.* There's a gap between what's offered and what the customer needs. In other words, the real problem doesn't get solved. It happens all the time. Call it tunnel vision, or design bias, or Ivory Tower Syndrome, or drinking our own bathwater. Whatever you call it, without a full grasp of the situation, we're innovating in the dark.

Cause: *The facts aren't clearly understood.* We think we understand the problem. We think we know what the customer wants. We look at reams of marketing reports. We conduct the focus groups. But we fail to descend into the field and take the long walk in the customer's boots. We don't even look over their shoulder while they struggle with the problem. And we take the customer's word at face value. It's not enough. *Telling* isn't *showing*.

Solution: *Learn to see.* See the forest *and* the trees. Live the customer's life. Watch the problem in the context and environment within which it occurs. View it from every conceivable angle. If you don't, you'll fail to properly frame the problem. You'll fail to empathize with your customers. There goes deep understanding. There goes innovation with impact.

The phrase in Japanese is *genchi genbutsu* (gen-chee-gen-boot-soo): go and see. Fully grasp the situation. See for yourself. Then, and only then, define the problem and design the appropriate solution.

The I in IDEA Loops

Whether you're solving an internal process problem, designing a new product or service, handling a customer relations challenge, or creating a new marketing campaign, the ability to understand the situation intimately is key to solving the problem elegantly. And that requires two things.

First, a thorough detective job. Taking a good hard look at the conditions surrounding the problem facilitates a complete investigation—the I in IDEA Loops. The goal is simple: *facts*.

Second, a deep dip in the customer experience. Maybe your customer is another department. Maybe it's an actual consumer. Your job is to move beyond the level of police detective to that of FBI profiler. The goal isn't easy: *Get inside the customer's mind.*

Perspective

It's hard to imagine a police criminalist processing evidence without collecting clues at the scene of the crime.

If the proliferation and popularity of television shows about criminal, scientific, and medical investigation is any indication, we have a real appetite for watching evidence and information be collected and analyzed.

Question: Why don't we engage in the same level of investigation in our efforts to solve problems and innovate?

Answer: It takes effort.

It's hard work. It requires mucking about in the sticks and weeds. That means getting your hands dirty.

Eyes Wide Open

Data is important. But it's not as important as facts and information. Data *indicates* facts, but it's not a substitute. It's *interpretation* that converts data into information. Enter the need to see the situation with your own eyes by getting out of your world and into that of the problem.

You have the best research report in the world? Great. Now go and confirm it for yourself. Allow your senses to absorb the qualitative side of the problem. Experience the environment. Gather the rich knowledge you can only get by immersing yourself in the physical circumstances.

Toyota believes so deeply and firmly in the practice of personal fact-finding and hands-on problem solving that *genchi genbutsu* is written in stone as one of the company's guiding values. It's not a strategy that's open to interpretation. It's not a sometimes thing practiced only when it's to one's advantage. It's a matter of operating principle.

They wouldn't abandon the practice even if they were penalized for it. That's how critical it is.

Toyota's stories of *genchi genbutsu* could fill a book. And it's not just a shop floor technique. Recall the Lexus story, in which the design team immersed themselves in the customer lifestyle and actually lived a luxurious life for a time? It's a perfect example.

> *We practice Genchi Genbutsu...go to the source to find the facts to make correct decisions, build consensus and achieve goals at our best speed.*
>
> **Toyota Motor Corporation**

It's practiced all the way to the boardroom. Hal Bracken, retired Toyota Motor Sales group vice president, tells this story:

"Dr. Shoichiro Toyoda, TMC president, was visiting dealers on the East Coast, accompanied by the regional manager and me. Dr. Toyoda was touring a dealership's service department when he noticed a Toyota on a lift with the automatic transmission removed. Dr. Toyoda turned to the dealership's service manager and through his translator asked, 'What's wrong with this car?'

"The service manager told Dr. Toyoda that they were having a problem with the transmission. Metal shavings were coming off the transmission case and getting into the valve body. Dr. Toyoda asked the service manager to show him the problem. The service manager walked Dr. Toyoda over to the transmission pan that had just been pulled and pointed to it.

"Dr. Toyoda looked at the pan. He was dressed in a dark suit with a white shirt and tie. He removed his coat and handed it to me. Then he rolled up his sleeves, stuck his hand into the pan, felt around in there and then came up with all these metal filings sticking to his fingers. He carefully placed a number of the shavings into his clean white handkerchief to save for future analysis in Japan and then proceeded to talk to his translator, who must have taken notes for ten minutes.

"I thought to myself, 'Wow, I could never imagine Lee Iacocca doing that!'"

LEARNING TO SEE: THE FIELD TACTICS

The value to innovation in learning to see lies in changing your perspective on the problem. Viewing the subject from every possible angle is a technique artists, sculptors, and photographers use regularly to enhance their ability to capture and render "the truth."

Learning to see sounds easier than it is. Yet more and more companies are beginning to understand just how important it is to successful innovation. It often provides the very inspiration required for elegant solutions.

At least three ways exist to fully grasp the situation. Each delivers a unique dimension of understanding. Toyota engages in all three.

1. Observe—watch the customer

2. Infiltrate—become the customer

3. Collaborate—involve the customer

Let's look at a few cases and stories of each.

1. Observe—Watch the Customer

• Under the leadership of CEO A. G. Lafley, Procter & Gamble has now shifted away from the sterile laboratory approach to product design taken by his predecessors. Scientists and designers now spend many hours of quality time with homemakers, observing how they go about the daily rigors of keeping house—how they vacuum a carpet, scrub the floor, diaper an infant, and do the laundry.

> Women don't care about our technology, and they couldn't care less what machine a product is made on. They want to hear that we understand them.
>
> **A. G. Lafley,** CEO
> Procter & Gamble

• When Levi-Strauss observed teenagers were driving cars over brand new jeans and then washing them with bleach, they began selling stone-washed, pre-faded jeans. Every new Levi's style comes from watching customers: women's only, pre-torn, relaxed, baggy, preshrunk.

• Car designers for Hyundai Motor America spend their Saturdays mingling at impromptu weekend classic car shows to not only get a glimpse of ageless design detail but also to get creative inspiration for their own work.

• Former Toyota Motor Sales president Jim Press initiated "fireside" chats with Lexus dealers when he ran Toyota's Lexus Division. According to Jim: *"I traveled the entire country with no agenda other than to listen, understand, and respect the insights and perspectives of our business partners. These meetings played a key role in establishing the relationships needed to get real feedback about market conditions and to get support for our market actions needed to achieve our division goals."*

• Product researchers for a facial tissue company asked a consumer panel to use their product in slow motion, describing as they did what they were doing, why they were doing it, and what they were thinking and feeling.

2. Infiltrate—Become the Customer

• To make sure they understood their target market, product developers for Toyota's new youth-oriented brand Scion attended raves and hip-hop parties. They came to understand that personal expression is the most powerful purchase motivation among Generation Y. They came to understand the trend in customization. Designers made sure to create a vehicle that enabled and encouraged buyers to add their signature and make it their own. Scion has now become a "raving" success with the younger crowd. The $15,000 Scion xB is scooped up as soon as it hits the dealer's lot, and the Gen Y crowd promptly pours thousands into the car—rims, sound systems, carbon trim, flat-panel screens. In one area of Southern California, Saturday morning sees an empty lot lined with xBs, back hatches open to display the custom handiwork.

• During their first week of job orientation at Toyota Motor Sales's corporate headquarters, management trainees are sent on mystery shopping excursions to automotive dealerships in order to understand the car-buying experience from the customer's perspective.

• When Harley-Davidson sales dropped in the mid-1980s, CEO Vaughn Beals directed his senior management team to attend biker rallies and go on all the big Harley rides. Vice president of design Willie Davidson, grandson of the founder, saw that every Harley had been customized. He took the modification ideas and adapted them to future designs—sculpting gas tanks, chopping the chassis, adding chrome, and painting flames.

• A senior executive heading the China operations for Tyson Foods walked through the streets of Shanghai, sampling the wares of the street vendors, in search of an exotic flavor authentically Chinese. One stand in particular stood out from the rest—a cart selling cumin-coated barbecued lamb on a skewer. That was the inspiration for an all new Tyson offering: cumin-flavored chicken strips. The new recipe was developed quickly and taste-tested to a 90% approval rating. Within three months the new product was on shelves.

• When design firm IDEO tackles a problem, the first thing they do is assemble a team chosen from both IDEO and the client company to observe and document the customer experience. A favorite practice is to have senior executives be a customer and shop for their own products or services in a variety of ways, as well as shop the competition. Many organizations, including Procter & Gamble, send their people to IDEO simply to learn to see. IDEO immediately sends them shopping. The goal: understand the consumer experience in order to innovate.

> They [IDEO] opened our eyes to new ways of working.
> **Claudi Kotchka,** VP
> Design Innovation, P&G

• Home Depot has since the early 1990s required outside board members of its board of directors to spend at least one day a year with senior executives and middle managers in both corporate and field functions. As with all *genchi genbutsu* activities, directors come to better understand the daily business issues, gain insight into the performance of the chief executives, and identify high potential managers to be groomed for the upper ranks.

3. Collaborate—Involve the Customer

• Designers at Whirlpool know that customers can't always articulate the problem that needs solving, so they study their products as they're used in the home. In a usability session involving a new refrigerator design, three separate cameras captured the difficulties in finding and replacing the water filter. Stop-action and slow-motion review of customer movement led designers to the solution. Not only do Whirlpool designers watch and videorecord the action in the kitchen, but they accompany technicians on service calls to gain insight into quality and dependability.

• In response to the deluge of customer suggestions, office-supply market leader Staples holds an annual office product design contest. The winner gets $25,000 and the opportunity to make and market the innovation under the Staples brand. Recent winners include a combination lock that uses letters rather than numbers, a handstrap stapler that fits in the palm for stapling paper to the wall, and oversized rubber bands with labels.

• Dell Inc.'s expansion beyond personal computers has led the company to regularly employ the kind of usability labs long utilized by consumer products makers. Involving the customer in the design of its Dell Pocket DJ mp3 player resulted in several enhancements, including repositioning an easy-to-use dedicated volume control and the use of brushed aluminum to minimize fingerprints and maximize the authentic feel of metal.

• Intuit's "Follow Me Home" program allows software designers of the personal finance package Quicken to observe first-time users as they install and set up the program. By sitting with the user in his or her home or office, designers gain understanding far beyond what they could from a sterile user-lab test. They learn what other programs reside on the person's hard drive, how navigation between those various applications works or doesn't work, and what paper and electronic sources of data the user pulls from to input into Quicken. Incorporating many of the resulting customer ideas and configuration suggestions led to the development of various targeted versions of the software.

> *Consumer adoption is driven much more by understanding the customer's psychology than it is by technology. The technology is there, what's missing is an understanding of how customers actually think and work.*
> **Scott Cook,** Founder, Intuit

NYPD Learns to See

Excellent power of observation is critical to police work. In a relatively new and unique program aimed at improving that ability, the New York Police Department sends recently promoted officers to the Frick Museum in Manhattan. The technique isn't as strange as it first appears. Solving crimes successfully requires careful attention to both detail and the bigger picture in order to find the connections and patterns between seemingly unconnected clues. NYPD enlisted the help of the Frick's education department to teach detectives how to examine a painting in detail in order to decipher the broader context of artistic intent. Limiting the examination time to a short span replicating the initial scan and quick analysis required on arrival at an actual crime scene, officers are required to describe the who, what, where, when, how, and why of paintings by the likes of Turner, Titian, Rembrandt, Hogarth, Vermeer and El Greco. The officers are taught to analyze an entire canvas. The process is one first of observation and description, moving from foreground to background, followed by analysis and conclusion.

How does that apply to assessing a crime scene? By widening the circle of observation to include a broader perimeter, detectives consider a wider range of clue sources to examine.

ToolKit: Learning to See

The New York Police Department is on to something. The following exercise was conducted at the Getty Museum on three separate occasions with different managers of a small Southern California company. Participants reported that not only did they believe their powers of observation improved, but also that they gained a new appreciation for personal artistry. Eyes and minds opened!

Visit an art museum or gallery with a colleague. Take a journal or notebook, and something to write with. Divide and conquer—go separate ways. You'll come back together at the end. Select any painting or work of art that strikes you as interesting, but preferably one containing people. Here's the assignment:

> *Step 1: Describe.* Scrutinize the painting. Working from the foreground to the background, describe in detail what you see. Refrain from interpreting or concluding. Your goal is to record the facts.
>
> *Step 2: Inquire.* Ask and answer the who, what, where, when, how, and why of the work. Who is the person in the scene? What is their story? What are they doing and why? Where is the scene taking place?
>
> *Step 3: Conclude.* Based on your description and inquiry, use your notes to draw conclusions and weave the story of the artwork.

Now get back together with your colleague and compare notes. What would they have concluded based on your description? What would you have concluded from their description?

IVORY TOWER PERILS

In any business, failing eyesight can be devastating. In fact, one of history's greatest blunders can be traced to the ivory tower peril of basing strategic innovation solely on prevailing market assumptions and consumer research reports.

We're talking about the Ford Edsel. It's the stuff of legend, but much of it wrong. As the story goes, the Edsel was simply a big risk that didn't pay off. Not true. The Edsel failed because Ford Motor couldn't see what was going on in the marketplace. They couldn't see, because they didn't bother to *go and see.*

> *Glance is the enemy of vision.*
> **Ezra Pound**

The 1957 Ford Edsel was meticulously planned. The depth of information used to design and market the vehicle was unparalleled. Body styling hit all the preferences confirmed by consumer research. The degree of quality control used to produce the Edsel was unprecedented.

The problem was, all the research was based on a forty-year-old market belief, originated by Alfred Sloan in the 1920s and around which General Motors was structured, that buyers fell into one of four income segments: low, low-middle, upper-middle, and upper. The Edsel was targeted for the upper-middle segment, both because it was the fastest growing segment and because Chrysler had vulnerability there.

Except the market didn't think that way. When it came to cars, consumers were thinking "lifestyle," not income. Ford hadn't gone to the field to see what was actually happening. They remained in the office and believed the data. Big mistake. The Edsel was dead on arrival, a complete and utter failure.

It was the postmortem investigation, the hansei, that not only told the story of the shift in market dynamics, but also, and more important, led to the immediate follow-up product considered by most to be one of the true breakthrough innovations in the automobile industry: the 1957 Ford Thunderbird.

The lesson is pretty clear. Always, always, go and see.

HANSEI

What solutions are your customers seeking?

How well do you understand the problem your customers face?

How do you experience what customers do?

How do you hear the customer's voice?

What part do customers play in solution design?

CHAPTER 6

Design for Today

There is nothing more powerful than an idea whose time has come.
Victor Hugo

Focus on Clear and Present Needs, or Your Great Ideas Remain Just That

Problem: *Solutions land far before the need.* Our best laid plans for the big idea fall short of their promise. Customers don't understand, because the solution doesn't fit any need they have. The idea is so futuristic that even typically early adopters are afraid or confused.

Cause: *Preoccupation with invention.* We become enamored of our brilliant ideas we believe will change the world, failing to consider the clear and present needs of the world as we know it today as thoroughly as we should. We mistake invention for innovation, with the missing link being the principle of *fit with society.*

Solution: *Design for today.* If you're trying to lead the market, make sure you're concentrating on a real need. Toyota calls it *market-in.* Don't confuse an unarticulated need with a nonexistent one. Don't attempt to manufacture a need. And don't confuse long lead times with future needs. The incubation and design period of the hybrid automobile lasted many years, but Toyota would have never even begun product development for an innovation that did not, if successful, have immediate application as a solution to a transportation need already in existence.

While a specific solution may take years or even generations to reach maturity, successful innovation requires a keen eye for capitalizing on immediate opportunities and a penchant for addressing current problems.

ACT TODAY FOR TOMORROW

The irony of designing solutions for today is that in reality you're acting today for tomorrow. Meaning the future. You've discovered a need that hasn't been met. It's a recognizable yet not obvious need, or the solution would be out there already. Most likely it's an unspoken need. When you're able to meet that need, you look like a visionary. That's part of what makes an elegant solution so, well, elegant. It's so very fitting.

> Don't try to innovate for the future. It's not enough to be able to say "In 25 years there will be so many very old people that they will need this."
>
> **Peter Drucker**

The mistake often made is one of timing. Timing your market is as difficult and perhaps as fruitless as timing the stock market. The difficulty comes in the fact that the primary forces of market structure, societal shift, and demographic movement are unpredictable. Many companies take what they think is the safe road, which is usually one of two extremes: yesterday's news or tomorrow's fantasy. Either way, they're out of luck. The market moves on, and the "tried and true" is now passé. The market heads south when you've gone north, and your "all brand new" offering is out in left field.

You're better off sticking with the three principles of innovation over the long haul. In other words, the Warren Buffett "buy and hold" method of investing in the stock market, over the day trader, technical market timing method. The Toyota way.

The good news is that market, societal and demographic shifts all have extremely long lead times until they hit. So if you do your due diligence by utilizing the kinds of practices in this book and exploited by Toyota, you too can realize the kind of long-term success they have.

You'll be spot-on in the delivery of high impact solutions.

INNOVATION BY DESIGN

The business press has for some time trumpeted the outsourcing of innovation by some of the biggest names on the corporate A-list: the likes of Dell, Motorola, and Phillips. And that's bad news. When you ship out innovation, all that's left is, ironically, a shipping department. By outsourcing, you're basically paying someone else to develop the invaluable intellectual capital you'll never own.

Toyota has a different take on design than a lot of firms. They keep it in-house. It's a matter of principle—*ingenuity in craft*—which finds its power in the words of Sakichi Toyoda himself: *"You can't be creative and complete a piece of work, unless, above all, you work on the construction yourself, attend carefully to every detail and experiment over and over again. And you must never leave the production to anyone else. These are the lessons I learned from experience, and they should be minded."*

When Toyota was developing a business case for hybrid technology in the 1990s, the decision was made to keep everything in-house. Design through assembly, from scratch. The obvious downside was the huge initial investment and the massive drain on the design and engineering labor pool. Recovery and return on investment would be a long time in coming, requiring exceptional commitment and patience.

The upside is now undeniable. Ten years later, Toyota is in the enviable position of not only having recovered their investment and realized market dominance in hybrids, but of having the ability to leverage their technology to accelerate design of the electric-hydrogen hybrid fuel cell. Toyota is one of only two automakers with wholly-proprietary fuel-cell technology.

Toyota's hybrid technology and youth market strategies prove the point. The $20,000 Prius hybrid and $15,000 Scion xB are among the most successful programs in the market today.

Toyota designs for today by exploiting change. Let's see how.

Exploiting Market Shifts: Hybrid Technology

It's a spectacularly entertaining time in the automotive industry as we watch Detroit's Big 3 do the hybrid shuffle. They were caught absolutely flat-footed by Toyota's foray into gas-electric hybrid technology. Business drama just doesn't get any better. Here's how it all started.

Perspective

Necessity is the mother of invention. OK. But great innovation needs a father: great timing. Inventors recognized the future need for electric light and power long before Thomas Edison invented the lightbulb, and spent many years working on fruitless ideas.

Edison waited for the immediate opportunity to become real, then marshaled his resources toward a successful concentrated effort of just a few years.

Design Dangers

#1: Creating a Future Need

Do people really need a chocolate lounge, à la Starbucks for coffee? Doubtful. But Mars believes if you build it, they will come. They're betting big that chocolate will be the new coffee. So they're launching "Ethel's Chocolate Lounge" nationwide. Raise your hand if you have the immediate and overwhelming need to linger over a plate of premium chocolate instead of a warm latte on the way to work. Perhaps Mars, Inc. is reading U.S. obesity statistics and popularity of diets differently. Perhaps it's simply a matter of Starbucks envy. A Mars executive was quoted as saying, "You see an attorney and his administrative assistant both standing in line to splurge on a four-dollar cup of coffee, why not chocolate?"

Mars might take a lesson from Gucci, who has recently reversed the "designer knows best" bias in favor of actually understanding what customers want. Of course, it took a Unilever executive schooled in ice cream marketing to do it, one Robert Polet, who took over the helm of Gucci recently and is turning it around.

#2: Confusing Need with Lead Time

What is a long lead time? Try thirty years. When your goal is to design and manufacture an artificial, implantable human heart, two or three decades is just about right. That's the ultimate mission of the AbioCor, a heart implant made by Abiomed that is just now realizing some medical success. The journey began in the mid-1970s, and the company founders knew that the development phase would be decades in the making, certainly longer than any other medical device that has entered clinical practice. When Abiomed began, the technology simply didn't exist. They knew it would be a generation before needed technologies would converge. So Abiomed developed lesser technologies along the way, each of which became a successful business helping millions of patients: an artificial heart valve, a cardiac-arrest system, an intra-aortic balloon pump.

The pressing need for an artificial human heart has always been there. Had it been developed thirty years ago, it would have had immediate clinical application.

Lesson: Don't confuse need with lead time.

When Toyota debuted its new hybrid Prius at the Kyoto Conference on global warming in December 1997, Detroit was utterly astonished. The Prius was far beyond concept and production-ready—it was in production. Delegates were offered rides in the several new Prius models on site. With half the CO_2 emissions and twice the fuel economy, the Prius garnered high interest and acclaim. According to those in attendance, the Big 3 affiliates at the conference were visibly shaken. Japan had committed to a 20% reduction in CO_2 emissions by 2010, while the United States had refused to commit at all. The Prius was launched immediately following the conference. The timing was impeccable.

> From the standpoint of business management, reading the times is important.
> **Eiji Toyoda**

One month later at the media opening for the Detroit Auto Show, a reporter confronted GM chairman Jack Smith on GM's EV1, a diesel hybrid to be production-ready by 2001. His question to Smith: Why would GM have the car only production-ready, not in consumers' hands by 2001, when Toyota's hybrid had already hit the streets to a great reception? Smith responded: "That depends on how we can prepare the infrastructure, how we deal with cost issues, and also what kind of public support we can get. In Japan, there is a technological subsidy system..." Toyota, in fact, received no government subsidy to develop the Prius.

Toyota's decision to pursue eco-friendly alternative energy systems had begun nearly a decade earlier in 1990, when Eiji Toyoda issued the challenge of taking action immediately to restructure Toyota's entire approach to research and development by saying, "I doubt that Toyota will survive in the twenty-first century without changing its way of doing R & D." The resulting shift away from model-based research represented the single greatest restructuring in the company's history. Advanced Energy Development was one of four new technological centers to emerge from the move.

Two themes surfaced in early brainstorming sessions: "Natural Resources" and "Environment." Toyota was acutely attuned to these two vital issues facing the planet, and finding solutions to these questions became the critical task for engineers and designers. In 1993, the decision was made to focus on developing an automobile that would reflect the very real environmental concerns while keeping all the advantages of conventional gasoline models.

"Toyota Earth Charter" had been founded the year before. It represented a detailed action index of Toyota's social contribution efforts—including environmental initiatives—in every stage of operations, from design and engineering to production, distribution, and disposal. It was above and beyond the call of duty, but in keeping with Toyota's core values. It was never publicized.

> Rather than just discussing the environment, we must present an ideal model that is sustainable into the future.
> **Hiroshi Okuda**
> Chairman, Toyota

Fast-forward to the end of 1996, when Toyota's then-president Hiroshi Okuda decided to make Toyota's efforts to promote a cleaner earth more visible. So was launched the ECO Project with the tagline: "Act Today for Tomorrow."

The following year, the Prius was launched at the Kyoto Conference. Earlier that year, Okuda had taken the stand at the "Toyota Environmental Forum" on the Tokyo waterfront to say: "Humans vested their dreams on automobiles in the twentieth century. For the automobile to sustain its position as a useful tool in the twenty-first century, the auto industry itself must lead society by making environmental efforts. Toyota will position preservation of the global environment as the top priority issue, and will allocate all necessary resources in our commitment."

Too bad the Big 3 didn't see it that way. Detroit failed to design for today. They were stuck in time and ignorant of the future, refusing to acknowledge an unarticulated market need. They didn't have to get left behind, they chose to. Ford, GM, Chrysler, and Honda all began researching alternative energy vehicles around the same time Toyota did. In fact, William "Bill" Ford, now Ford's CEO, was one of the attendees at Kyoto who was taken for a spin in the new Prius in 1997. The Big 3 participated in a $1.2 billion government project sponsored by the Clinton administration called the Partnership for a New Generation of Vehicles to find a breakthrough automobile that could achieve 80 miles per gallon. The conclusion of the General Accounting Office in 2000: *"An adequate market for a lighter-weight, fuel-efficient vehicle does not currently exist, nor is it expected to develop in the near future."* Whoops.

The reality was that the then-dominant trend toward SUVs and trucks made Detroit profit-blind to other market shifts developing with longer lead times. Executives collectively said that consumers prefer larger trucks, which are heavier and less fuel-efficient. They failed to understand the market fully, because they couldn't see the broader context. Or were trying to outsmart potentially stricter efficiency standards. Either way, they were, in effect, designing for yesterday.

And the hits just keep coming. Today, Detroit publicly whines about Toyota's lead, going as far as to say that Toyota's approach is, at least according to one Ford executive referring to the scarce supply of parts, "predatory." When your competitor is eating your lunch, or eating you *for* lunch, a statement like that is understandable.

Exploiting Demographic Shifts: The Scion Story

The story of Scion, Toyota's new youth brand, makes it clear how critical it is to take action today to ensure tomorrow. If you're Toyota, you know that your prime consumer base is aging, being replaced by the 60 million-strong Generation Y crowd, the so-called millennials, kids of Generation X. The 8-to-23-year-olds who will absolutely dominate global sales by 2020. The thinking went something like this.

One thing the Toyota and Lexus brands aren't: youthful. No matter what we say or do, we can't escape that fact of life. We know because we've tried to market to the younger generation, and they're not buying it. They think differently. They don't like marketing. They like to discover things on their own. They like to be different. We're shooting for 15% of the total car market by 2010, so we need something just for them.

We have to make it completely, radically different. It has to reflect the lifestyle. And we need it now. It can't be a Toyota—can't look, feel, or drive like one. The product is everything for the young people. It's got to be hip. Out there, but not way out: customizable, with strong emotional appeal. It's got to say...no, it screams, "I'm new!" Do we have such a thing?

> We have to clearly realize that if we are not aware of...changes and stick to old ideas, we may get left behind.
> **Shotaro Kamiya**
> Former President, TMS

Yes. In Japan. It's a concept called the bB. Engineer Tetsuya Tada has been working on it for two years. They say it's fun to drive.

Designer Genes

Hunter's Rules for Innovation by Design

Kevin Hunter heads CALTY, one of Toyota's three major design centers, located in Newport Beach, California. CALTY is involved in nearly all of Toyota's major vehicle design programs. According to Kevin, Toyota wants constant movement forward, and design plays an enormous role in that effort. Design is the face of innovation. He has a few rules for the road warriors in his company that have been hardwired now as guidelines.

Rule #1: *Balance today and tomorrow.* "People can't tell you what they want in the future," says Kevin. "But they know what they want now. You have to balance creativity with market acceptability. You have to push the envelope and be progressive, but you can't get too far out there, because customers won't understand. Your design has to evoke something familiar or emotional while at the same time offering something new and unfamiliar." He adds, "You have to avoid a strict design bias and remember who you're designing for. You can't be selfish, you must focus outward, and on the problem you're trying to solve for customers."

Rule #2: *Keep it real and resonant.* Kevin states that "there's a sense of urgency to make design count, to resonate with the buyer." He believes you can never stand still. The customer is always moving, changing, and if you're not out there all the time trying to understand the functional and emotional needs of consumers, your design will simply fall flat.

Rule #3: *Blend creativity and competition.* "We take creative contribution very seriously," Kevin notes. "It's part of every performance review and looked at closely from an evaluation perspective. We work as a team, but it's always overlaid with intense competition for the winning ideas. For every design, we have a number of smaller teams in the hunt. To make creativity flow and give people the freedom to think, we've removed much of the layering that other organizations have. Hierarchy stifles innovation, and we need open and honest disagreement about every idea. Every idea counts!"

It's got an unusual look to it: almost square. Okay, it's a little weird. That's a good thing, because these kids are all about "look at me" and "listen to this." The back opens up wide—perfect—the kids can jam everything they want in there, every sound component known to man. They can make it all their own. Excellent, they love to customize. It's cheap, $15,000, so they can afford it, and still have some left over for the bling-bling. We're not wild about the name...xB is better. And we need a hatchback version with a little more curve. And a coupe later on down the road.

We've got 18 months to create a brand from scratch. We have to keep costs low. The budget's small. That's OK, we're not advertising in a big way. But we won't need to, we know Gen Y hates ads, hates the push. In fact, we're going to keep it quiet.

Options, they like options. They're Web-heads, so we need mp3 and satellite. The cars need to be wired for everything. Oh, and we need one more thing: all new cars every four years. Not just face-lifts. New models, or this won't work. It'll be a flash and poof, they're on to the next. So start working on that today. Stay nimble, stay quick, stay flexible. This crowd moves fast and if we don't keep up with them, we're out. Get this right and we won't have to fret about scrambling to react to big consumer shifts ever again. We'll know what to do and how to do it.

Where are these kids going to buy the car? There's no time or money for new stores. That's a problem. That means they go to a Toyota store. Okay, so they'll know it's a Toyota. How do we get around that? Think! We don't. It's not the ugly stepchild. It's legit, but different. It's Scion, offspring of Toyota. Don't ignore the Toyota link, it's got cred. These kids are better than we were when it comes to respecting elders. They're better educated than we were. With these kids if you act like a poser, you'll get treated like a poser. Idea: Make it so they bypass the Toyota part and go to a special center. Scion only. Make the place cool. Distinctly Scion: no Toyota product allowed, Web-wired, now tunes, low-key. Keep the sales guys back, but train them well—they need to know everything there is to know, because these kids are smart. We use online configuration. We fix the price, so there's no haggle. We offer plenty of options, but no upselling. We use pure pricing—it is what it is. No pressure.

How do we market this thing? We go low-profile. We take it to the streets. We let them discover it on their own, get the buzz going. We display at raves. We display at urban art tours. We get it into DUB magazine. It'll work.

And work it did. Unbelievably well. But it had to. The platform was burning, at least in the minds of Toyota executives. The 50-year-old Toyota customer was soon going to be replaced by a 20-something buyer who was everything a Toyota buyer wasn't: brand-sensitive, ethnically diverse, seeking fun and entertainment, difficult to reach, techno-savvy, well-connected, discriminating and demanding, with a decent disposable income and strong sense of entitlement.

In one sense, Scion represented a completely new way of doing business, aligned to the new buyer. In another sense, it was not as great a leap as outside observers have made it appear. The looming demographic shift was well known. Toyota had learned a lot about Gen Y through their Genesis strategic youth marketing program. Ideas about new retail practices, including one-price selling, had been around for years. A fitting product was already being developed for the Japanese market. More than anything, Scion was an eclectic composition of several smaller efforts synthesized to become a new business model capable of taking Toyota into tomorrow.

Scion effectively reinvented Toyota.

What's significant about that is the *timing*. Most reinvention occurs at rock bottom. Toyota's happened at the peak of their success. You can count on one hand the number of large organizations that have successfully accomplished that.

When in 1999 Yoshimi Inaba took the helm of Toyota Motor Sales, U.S.A., he took a critical look at the social situation and issued the challenge of addressing the youth market. Said Inaba: *"The*

The Gray Market

Gen Y is just one demographic shift to exploit. On the other side of the spectrum lies the growing percentage of the population considered elderly, seeking custom mobility solutions. Sure, Japan's population is aging quickly, with 25% expected to be 65 or older by 2015. But no other carmaker caters to the older generation as extensively as does Toyota, with nearly 40 different models converted to accommodate things like wheelchairs and walkers, with features such as automatic doors, curtains, and swivel seats. Toyota has been working on innovations with the graying market in mind since the early 1990s, when then-Chairman Shoichiro Toyoda decided that Toyota had a responsibility to serve the aging and began encouraging senior managers to make the elderly a company-wide priority.

number-one enemy of TMS was its own success. It was even more Toyota-like than TMC. I called it a 'conventional model at its prime.' It was easy for us to try to avoid anything that might disturb TMS, since TMS was doing so well and contributing a significant amount of profit to Toyota."

Avoidance was not an option. Toyota's clarion call would be to innovate and act today in order to meet and survive tomorrow.

IN THE NOW

Designing for today is the path to tomorrow. Innovation-challenged organizations make the fatal mistake of thinking they can create a future need by designing a futuristic product or service. So they overshoot the mark and wait for the customer to show up. That's a risky wait, because it rarely happens as hoped, and the cost of capital is huge and punitive.

Meanwhile, their version of designing for today is in reality yesterday's design, because the customer keeps moving forward. They land on the spot the customer just left, because they've refused to accept the current reality. They've seen it, confronted it, didn't like what they saw, and gone back into the burrow. That's the easiest thing in the world to do.

Designing for today requires a firm grasp of the market, society, and the customer. We need to know where they're headed. But don't expect them to tell us. They won't. We have to figure it out. The previous chapters showed how to do that. The good news is that the trend data is generally readily available. The parade is already in progress. All you need to do is get out in front of it.

The task is one of exploiting the market, societal, and demographic shifts occurring around you. They represent constant change. And huge opportunity for innovation. More important, since the events behind the shifts have already occurred, it's opportunity you can hang your hat on.

The requirement is paying sufficient attention, accepting facts perhaps contrary to your belief, and acting in the now to employ your best marksmanship. Failure to exploit the changing requirements of the market and customer is a failure to innovate.

Done right, the outcome of designing for today will materialize as the future wave you're looking for.

ToolKit: Ballistics

According to neuroscientist Dr. William Calvin, author of *Ascent of Mind,* we're hardwired with a natural ballistic prowess—the innate and uniquely human ability to throw an object and hit a moving target. Only humans have the genetic ability to think ahead, to project ourselves into the future, and to launch a plan of attack that hits the objective.

Designing for today is about developing that natural ballistic ability into business marksmanship.

Consider the following graphic. Where do your efforts lie? How well matched are your designs with changing customer requirements?

Shooting Practice:

- Identify the critical issue or decision. (Example: Should we develop hybrid technology?)

- List the uncontrollable forces—the market, societal, and demographic shifts—under way. List only those with factual evidence.

- Number and "map" the factors according to relevance using two characteristics: potential impact and certainty. Create a simple four-square matrix to plot impact versus certainty.

- Develop at least three scenarios, preferably four. That way you won't fall into the natural tendency to take the middle choice by default.

- Decide a course of action based on the three principles of innovation from Part 1.

Hansei

What is the pressing need your design meets?

How quickly can your idea be applied?

What market, societal, or demographic shifts can you exploit?

If your idea became a reality today, how well would it do?

How streamlined are your development cycles?

CHAPTER 7

Think in Pictures

The soul cannot think without a picture.
Aristotle

Make Your Intentions Visual—You'll Surprise Yourself with the Image

Problem: *The endgame isn't clear.* Or compelling. Or detailed. No one recognizes success because they don't know what it looks like. Without a vivid picture of the intended target, why it's urgent and important, and what things will look like when they get there, creative engagement in the innovation effort wanes. Without the best thinking being brought to the table by everyone, finding elegant solutions is impossible.

Cause: *Underdeveloped storytelling skill.* We shortchange the problem-solving effort by utilizing flat, sequential, fix-it thinking rather than weaving a multidimensional story of the ideal end-state. When we do get around to the bigger thinking, we get mired in the old linear thought process of writing emails, memos, tabular reports, and spreadsheets, thus depicting the desired future in a far too pedestrian way. Underachievement of goals is often traced to a glaring absence of a compelling mental image to guide the effort.

Solution: *Tell the story with pictures.* There's a reason everyone talks about "the big picture." So get graphic about it, literally or figuratively. Get visual: storyboard it, diagram it, mindmap it, whiteboard it, butcher-paper the walls, and go crazy. Show progress against your goals in an appealing, unboring way. Get vivid: Show people the gripping picture of the future by telling the story in a powerful way, using imagery to describe the goal.

PICTURE THIS

The value of mental imagery and visualization in driving performance is undisputed. Sustained leadership in most any realm hangs on it. We forget just how important it is to our everyday work, between all the busywork. We forget to keep our visual skills and tools sharp through constant use. Then we wonder why no one, including our customers, "gets the picture."

> *I must always have a clear image of the form of a work before I begin. Otherwise there is no impulse to create.*
> **Barbara Hepworth**

Howard Gardner, in his book *Leading Minds*, makes the point that leaders we consider "visionary"—be they artist, executive, or diplomat— have the ability to call up a mental image to deliver a compelling message around which people can rally. It takes a bit of the poet to add texture. A few well-known examples prove the point.

Walt Disney on Disneyland:

"...Disneyland...will be a place for people to find happiness and knowledge...a place for parents and children to spend pleasant times in one another's company; a place for teachers and pupils to discover greater ways of understanding and education. Here the older generation can recapture the nostalgia of days gone by, and the younger generation can savor the challenge of the future...Disneyland will be something of a fair, an exhibition, a playground, a community center, a museum of living facts, and a showplace of beauty and magic. It will be filled with the accomplishments, the joys and hopes of the world we live in. And it will remind us and show us how to make those wonders part of our lives."

Winston Churchill on Britain's finest hour:

"Hitler knows he will have to break us on this island or lose the war. If we can stand up to him, all Europe may be free, and the life of the world may move forward into broad, sunlit uplands. But if we fail, the whole world, including the United States, including all we have known and cared for, will sink into the abyss of a new Dark Age, made more sinister and perhaps more protracted by the lights of

perverted science. Let us therefore brace ourselves to our duties and so bear ourselves that if the British Empire and its Commonwealth last for a thousand years, men will say, 'This was their finest hour.'"

Henry Ford on the automobile:

"I will build a motor car for the great multitude...It will be so low in price that no man making a good salary will be unable to own one and enjoy with his family the blessing of hours of pleasure in God's great open spaces...When I'm through, everybody will be able to afford one, and everyone will have one. The horse will have disappeared from our highways, the automobile will be taken for granted and we will give a large number of men employment at good wages."

Martin Luther King Jr. on "the dream":

"I have a dream that one day on the red hills of Georgia the sons of former slaves and the sons of former slave owners will be able to sit down together at the table of brotherhood. I have a dream that one day even the State of Mississippi, a desert state sweltering in the heat of injustice and oppression, will be transformed into an oasis of freedom and justice. I have a dream that my four children will one day live in a nation where they will not be judged by the color of their skin but by the content of their character. I have a dream today..."

Pictures and images connect people to the intention in a very forceful way, touching hearts and minds. They connect the right brain with the left and help us see the path more clearly. They provide valuable travel hints that let us chart the way to the future with confidence. Visual reference plays a big part in virtually every aspect of business. It figures into everything Toyota does, from high level strategies to design sketches to production visual controls.

No treatment of the use of visuals would be honest or effective without the use of images, so the remainder of this chapter will be just that: stories, tools, and examples of how thinking in pictures is actually used, and why it plays such a critical role in innovation.

Words are but pictures of our thoughts.
John Dryden

As Napoléon said, a picture is worth a thousand words.

Creating Tomorrow by Painting Today

Kerry Morrison was the underdog candidate for the executive directorship of the Hollywood Entertainment District business improvement district (BID), a sorely needed urban renewal effort devoted to reversing the nearly half-century decline of the landmark community. In fact, the board had all but decided on another candidate. That is, until Kerry walked into the room in 1996 and painted a realistic picture of how Hollywood appeared to outsiders. Her vivid description created the proper context for action.

Doing business every day in Hollywood, the board was too close to the problem and couldn't quite see the depth of the crisis with objective clarity. It took an outsider with a keen eye for the truth and an artist's ability to render a compelling image.

Kerry had nothing to lose. So she told it like it was. She described her drive in to Hollywood that day. How all the debris blown up against the blocks of chain-link fence lining subway construction sites had rattled her. How the urban street denizens had made her feel nervous walking from the remote parking lot to the interview. How the blight of decaying buildings hid what had once been the most magnificent boulevard in Los Angeles. How she couldn't find a decent place to find a quick lunch among the iron-gated closed-down stores and boarded-up shops. How the scene was even worse than she had remembered from her last visit some fifteen years ago. And how never in the present day would she even fleetingly consider bringing her young children to Hollywood.

As the president of the board listened to her, he sat back in his chair to appraise Kerry. Numb from the four other interviews that day, he knew at that moment he had found the right champion of a most important cause.

Over the course of the next ten years, the original picture would change. Many factors, projects, and leaders contributed to the Hollywood Renaissance, but the BID was the foundation. Slowly and with great difficulty, the masterpiece of realism drove daily progress. The Morrison family moved into the area, and from a donated windowless office without so much as a phone on the first day of her new job, Kerry set about the Herculean task of implementing the goals articulated by the property owners who had hired her.

Creating the future meant making the city first and foremost clean and safe. It started with six city blocks. But visible success from the cleanup tripled the project size. Things began to snowball. More and more property owners came onboard, increasing the budget significantly. Crime dropped dramatically. Subway stations opened. Buildings got face-lifts. Street corners got new life. Nightlife returned. Golden era hotels and theaters were renovated and reopened. Within five years, the evidence was clear that a new reality had indeed been achieved.

When in 2002 the Academy Awards returned to Hollywood after a decades-old absence, Kerry knew that Hollywood had found its tipping point.

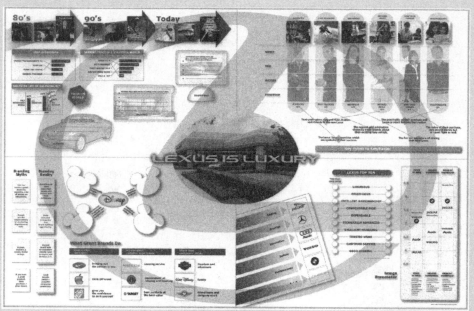

Image courtesy of University of Toyota.

Visual Strategy

Strategies come and go, as they should in a shifting marketplace. Without a way to cut through the myriad of different strategic initiatives all taking place at the same time, the average corporate citizen becomes a bit immune to the latest, greatest program. To ensure that every associate around the country understood the new strategic brand direction, Lexus conducted a multimedia educational immersion experience. Part of the program utilized a large table-sized visual split among the quadrants, each component focusing on a different aspect of the brand strategy and allowing each participant to discover the new direction through interactive exercises. The process enabled people to more quickly invest their thinking around the brand in a creative, visually stimulating, and nonsequential way. Key ideas were more thoroughly embraced and remembered because they weren't hidden in a densely worded strategic document. Relationships between high-level concepts were more easily seen and understood, without the need for exhaustive explanation. The method resulted in a stronger connection to the strategy and thus more cohesive and focused execution.

Mapping Strategy to Action

Visual Display of Data, from Napoléon to Toyota

The visual display of information allows you to map vision against action, pictorially connecting high- and line-level strategy with progress toward measurable targets.

Edward R. Tufte, who the *New York Times* once called "the Leonardo da Vinci of data," considers the famous centuries-old map below drawn by Charles Joseph Minard to be one of the finest statistical graphics ever produced. The map shows Napoléon's losses during the Russian campaign of 1812. Variables plotted include troop size, location, direction of movement, temperature, and time. The width of the thick upper band shows the size of Napoléon's army shrinking from 422,000 to 100,000 as it invaded Russia. The path of retreat during the bitter cold winter is shown by the dark lower band. Only 10,000 troops returned to France. The bottom-most line charts temperature over time during the three-month retreat.

According to Tufte, the graphic tells a rich, coherent story far more enlightening than a single number plotted over time.

Legend has it that members of the Court of France broke down and wept when shown the diagram.

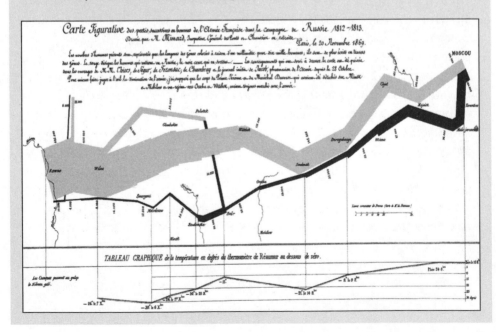

Creative Visual Control

Visual control is an integral part of Toyota's methodology. The Project Management Office of Toyota's North American Parts Operation (NAPO) used creative visual "dashboards" to track performance in their Stretch Goals initiative (see Chapter 9).

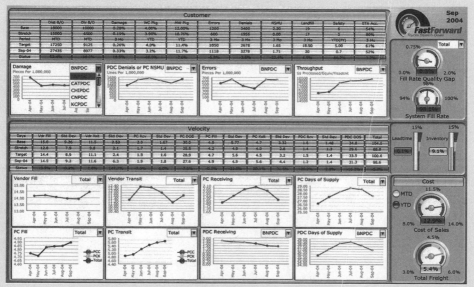

Images courtesy of NAPO. Note: Measures shown are for illustration only, and do not reflect actual data.

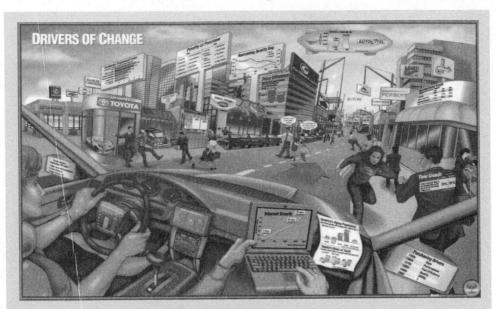

Getting the Big Picture Requires . . . a Big Picture

To enable associates to get a better perspective of the larger system to which they belong and the various forces shaping their business, Toyota uses a large pictorial board—called a Learning Map®—to provide a centerpiece for a guided discussion and exploration. Learning Maps® enhance systems thinking by providing a visual link between cause and effect in a single, fluid view.

Images courtesy of University of Toyota. Learning Map® is a registered trademark of Root Learning, Inc.

Obeya: The Wall of Work

Obeya (oh-bay-ya), which means "big room" in Japanese, is the nerve center for any Toyota team project. During the 1990s, then-president Fujio Cho became concerned with the decline in workplace collaboration due to the rise of email and videoconferencing. Cho required teams to once again work face-to-face in obeya. Obeya provides a designated forum for surfacing and solving problems, and is used in all aspects of Toyota's operations. The obeya is easily identified by the lack of available wall space. Diagrams, design, and engineering plans, problem-solving sheets, product issues—you name it, and it's up and visual. The "Wall of Work" displays current thinking around the given situation.

Output from obeya sessions, which can last from minutes to days, is visual and captured on a large tabloid-sized sheet nicknamed an A3, which refers to the international paper size. The A3 is Toyota's standard reporting mechanism to capture and tell a story in one continuous view. The advantage is that a clear and logical line of thinking is portrayed in a graphic format, connecting cause and effect in common methodology. Strategic plans, problem-solving reports, project proposals—all get told on the one-page A3. The thought is this: If you can't get your thinking on one page, you haven't really done your thinking. Besides, who wants to read 60 pages of PowerPoint slides, when one page will do the job?

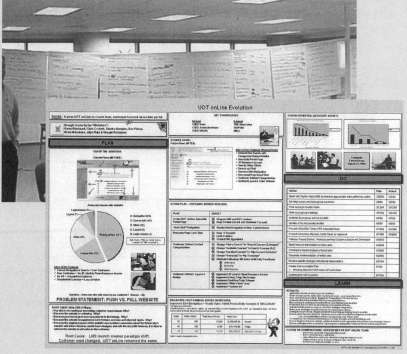

Images courtesy of University of Toyota

ToolKit: The 3-Hour Vision

Companies spend days in offsite retreats developing visions and strategies. Here's how it can be done on-site in a half-day session.

Rapid change within organizations causes rampant reorganization, in turn creating a huge need for on-the-fly gear shifting for teams and business units. The effectiveness of executive edict has for the most part disappeared in today's modern company, and without some way to bring everyone onboard to create collective mindshare and build a plan in real-time in a collaborative fashion, the emotional investment needed to ensure success just won't happen. So, how do you design and execute a half-day session that sets up the new leader, gets everyone on the same page, and charts a path for the foreseeable future?

One way is the "3-Hour Vision" meeting.

The University of Toyota used this technique to launch their strategy in 1999. The unconventional "corporate obituary" is preferred over the standard "success story" because it results in a much more realistically and vividly portrayed picture of perfection, albeit in reverse.

As a starting point, understanding what the goal or vision ISN'T is often more important than what it IS, because it outlines the restraining forces, which always rule. (See Chapter 9!) For most people, painting the disaster scene provides more readily accessible mental images, because they've seen them before at some point in their experience. When the roadblocks appear in the future, they are more easily recognized and effectively addressed.

AGENDA ITEM	TIMING	AGENDA ITEM
Leadership Message	*15 min*	Meeting kickoff; introductions; where we're going; what we will achieve
Vision Mapping: Headline News! Disaster Strikes!	*45 min*	Write the Corporate Obituary: What would the article say that describes your team's demise?
Removing Obstacles	*45 min*	Gain clarity on major outcomes: How will each obstacle be overcome or avoided?
Break	*15 min*	Break
Stretch Goals	*30 min*	Master list of objectives to get to the vision. (See Ch.9 for more on Stretch Goals.)
Goal Prioritization & Timing	*30 min*	Arrive at top five priorities through a democratic process.

ToolKit: Pinwheel Diagrams

Try This Brainstorming Aid to Map Ideas

You're in the design phase of an IDEA Loop. Instead of simply making a list of ideas, add another dimension to your thinking by using a pinwheel diagram to chart, connect, and build upon ideas and possible solutions.

All you need is some large blank paper and a few colored markers. Use standard brainstorming rules. First, shorthand your target or goal with some sort of picture, symbol or icon, circle it, and place it in the middle of the page. Next, as you brainstorm ideas and solutions, draw lines radiating outward from the center, labeling each with a separate idea or alternative. Use smaller lines off the larger one to note subordinate ideas.

Finally, note any connections, patterns, or themes by using dotted lines to join ideas.

In a fairly short time, you should have a working visual map of the various options for reaching the goal.

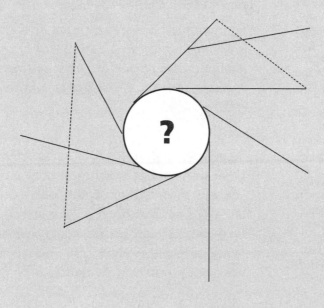

Exercise: Future Perfect

Vision is essential. We can't advance in any direction without it. To illustrate the point, stand up and lift one leg off the floor, and hold it there for ten seconds. That's easy. But now try it with your eyes closed. It's pretty tough to do!

Try this exercise on a regular basis in your problem solving to develop and maintain your visual skill:

Beyond Fix-It

A Fortune 500 company faced a workforce crisis. Sexual harassment claims were causing a tremendous loss in productivity. Training programs seemed to only make things worse. One day a close advisor asked, "What do you really want?" "To fix the situation," came the reply. "Really?" asked the advisor. "Show me. Draw it out."

As the CEO completed his rough sketch, he was surprised at what he saw—men and women working side by side, fully engaged in collaboration. He realized that just neutralizing a negative situation wouldn't get him that. What he really wanted was harmonious workplace relationships.

It wasn't too long before the company became a *Fortune* magazine "100 Best Companies to Work For."

Step 1. *Answer the question: "What do I really want?"*

Describe what you see as the ideal in your mind's eye, using a statement that begins with "I see..."

For example: *I see our department as setting the benchmark of effectiveness and efficiency in all of our operations in an effort to promote the stability needed to realize the highest levels of productivity, performance, and profitability.*

Step 2. *Create a statement of the end-state using the future perfect tense.*

For example: *Standardized work processes, policies, procedures, and tools are supported by the diligent administration of quality control and management, enabling internal operations to function at peak efficiency levels.*

Step 3. *Sketch what you have just described verbally.* Don't worry about artistry, just draw it out as best you can. Avoid using words, but an occasional one-word exclamatory (e.g., Victory!) is okay. Fill up the whole page. Use different colors of pen and pencil to make it vivid. Use symbols and icons whenever possible. Stick figures are okay!

GETTING GRAPHIC

Toyota chief engineer Tetsuya Tada used a high-energy, heart-pounding music video to propose the Scion concept to Toyota's senior executives.

At BMW-owned design studio Designworks USA in Southern California, all employees take art classes to improve and maintain their graphic ability, even if their main tool of choice is the computer.

> *No one is an artist unless he carries his picture in his head before painting it, and is sure of his method and composition.*
> **Claude Monet**

To provide a glimpse of their future facility, the University of Toyota produced a high-end, multimedia, computer-animated, virtual tour of the campus through the proposed classrooms, auditoriums, and *dojos* (training rooms) for dealership service technician training.

At Toyota's CALTY Design, car concepts begin with a hand-drawn sketch, progress to a computer-aided illustration, and eventually become small-scale clay models. Yes, they still make clay models. The computer can't replace the human element.

It seems the value of getting things into some sort of visual, graphic format is a critical component to successful innovation in any domain. The stories, examples, and tools in this chapter illustrate two important points about the practical use of pictures in solving problems.

1. *Pictures and images connect people to thoughts and goals and help turn valuable ideas into action.*

2. *There is no step-by-step process or one best way for thinking in pictures.*

Display data pictorially. Use photographs. Write fictitious articles. Make sketches. Use IDEA Briefs. Whenever you can, wherever you can, start building a visual element into your thinking.

You'll be surprised at the difference a picture makes.

HANSEI

How and where do you make use of mental images?

What images depict the desired state?

How well connected are people to your ultimate goal?

What opportunities exist to use images and visual references?

What does the ideal solution look like?

CHAPTER 8

Capture the Intangible

The qualities of art? First, it must be indescribable, and second, it must be inimitable.
Renoir

The Most Compelling Solutions Are Often Perceptual and Emotional

Problem: *Solutions lack that certain something.* Je ne sais quoi—literally, in French, "I don't know what." That indefinable, indescribable, inexpressible quality that makes the leader the leader. Products and services fail to differentiate themselves. Solutions are either too me-too, or too wannabe. We wonder why our competition is so far in the lead, when they sell essentially the same basic thing.

Cause: *Transaction tunnel vision.* Somehow we're missing the truth of what customers are really buying. We're too focused on the tangible exchange, the big deliverable. We're consumed with our solution's features, and advantages over the competition. We're blinded by the outcome, and we're ignoring the experience. So we're neglecting what the customer really wants. It's clearly not a product or service.

Solution: *Capture the intangible.* It's the intangibles that differentiate and transform. They move well beyond the transaction, the product, the service, the process. Capture the intangibles that people truly prize, and you'll find the most compelling elements of value. Lexus doesn't sell luxury transportation, it sells safe sanctuary and quiet escape. Disney doesn't operate theme parks, it sells magic and fantasy. And Starbucks doesn't sell coffee, it offers personal expression and daily ritual.

It's business art.

Soft-Side Value

The idea of perceptual, emotional, or otherwise intangible value in business can be traced back at least three generations to the Great Depression, when Cadillac effectively stopped selling automotive transportation. In the 1930s, Nicholas Dreystadt took over as the company was about to fail and announced that Cadillac did not compete with other automakers, but that *"Cadillac competes with diamonds and mink coats. The Cadillac customer does not buy transportation, but status."* That simple perceptual innovation translated to a price premium and saved the company. Within two years Cadillac had become a major growth business despite the dismal economy.

> *Emotion is an unlimited resource with unlimited power.*
> **Kevin Roberts,** CEO
> Saatchi & Saatchi

Status. Perceptual, yes. Emotional, yes. Intangible, absolutely. Soft and fuzzy, yet *real* value in the mind of the customer. And that's where it counts. Because when it comes to innovative, elegant solutions, the old cliché is true: perception is reality.

Make no mistake, we're not talking about branding. We're talking about an elevated view of value. Above and beyond the tangible deliverable, the commodity, and the deal. The tangible drivers of value—*quality, cost, speed*—are the ante to the game. To be a real player, you must absolutely get the transaction right. From a customer's point of view, though, the tangibles are simply a means to the end.

Intangible drivers of value get to the heart of what *motivates* purchase behavior. If you can answer the tougher questions of what tangibles *do* for the buyer—how speed improves life, what quality actually buys in the mind of the customer—you're entering the domain of intangible value. You transcend the mere economic transaction, because the emotional bonds that result are much stronger than the dollar exchange.

Answer them *correctly*, and deliver that answer to the customer, and the relationship rises to a whole new level. Intangibles are behind some of the great success stories in business.

Here's the thought: *It's not business, it's personal.*

It's Not Business, It's Personal

There's nothing new in the understanding that to build a profitable, long-term, close-knit relationship with the customer, you need to constantly connect on two levels, rational and emotional. One is tangible, the other is intangible.

Rational is bang for the buck. We all get that. *Emotional* is more about trust, caring, loyalty, respect...all the things we look for in a good partner. We don't always quite get that. At least not completely. But the emotional side of value can be a real inroad to innovation.

What makes the emotional connection so difficult to wrangle is the irrationality. You can't necessarily analyze it. Customers actually aren't that much help to you in defining it. They can't always tell you why they love what they love, at least in terms that are useful. Sometimes they just don't know. Sometimes they know exactly why, but don't want to tell you.

Because *it's personal.*

So how do you manage that? You deliver the personal touch. You do your best to understand human nature and how the mind works. Which is why Toyota has at times employed anthropologists, psychologists, and behavioral scientists, who consistently tell us that people buy for individual reasons linked to their personal values. And, significantly, that they buy because some internal compass tells them they should.

That internal compass points in one universal direction: *security.* Let's take a closer look at what that means.

The Role of Risk

The need to trust is born only out of our belief that we are somehow vulnerable. Trust goes hand in hand with, and is dependent on, a perceived risk. Without risk, there's simply no

> **Perspective**
>
> Kevin Roberts, Worldwide CEO of Toyota's long-time ad agency Saatchi & Saatchi, firmly believes that the emotional connection to customers transforms the brand and the business.
>
> His term for that level of connection is "lovemark."
>
> According to Kevin, attributes of the emotional connection number three: mystery, sensuality, and intimacy.
>
> Mystery refers to the stories, myths, and icons surrounding the business.
>
> Sensuality refers to the five senses of sight, sound, smell, touch, and taste.
>
> Intimacy refers to commitment, empathy, and passion.

need to talk about trust. That's the insight needed to provide a starting point on delivering the personal touch: People buy solutions to problems, and the one problem everyone shares is the problem of security, or insecurity, depending upon how you frame it.

It's all about risk!

Consumer behaviorist Ernest Dichter determined in the 1950s that most people perceive at least five dimensions of downside risk every time they engage in a purchase experience:

- *Economic*—Will this waste my money?
- *Functional*—Will this work reliably well?
- *Social*—What will others think of me?
- *Physical*—Will this somehow be painful?
- *Psychological*—Will I think poorly of myself?

This insight makes the whole issue of delivering intangible value a little more accessible. Understanding that at the heart of everything people are buying some form of security makes framing the problem much easier. We can see why quality and consistency count, because they make us feel safe. We can see why price counts, because it makes us feel intelligent. We can see why design counts, because it makes us look good. We can begin to see why outfits like Starbucks, Lexus, Apple, Disney, and JetBlue stand out.

> *Many of our actions are motivated by a conflict between security and change, which often spells insecurity.*
> **Ernest Dichter**

When we tap into the security zone, we begin to build the kind of collaborative partnership we seek with customers.

Let's see how it plays out in the real world of business.

STUFF WE LOVE

Love is a pretty strong word. But it's probably the most powerful emotion we know. Certainly the most positive. Hearing a customer say they love what you have to offer is what it's all about. Nothing speaks louder.

Emotion By Design
The Pottery Barn 3-Step

Designers at Pottery Barn firmly believe that emotionally, every product has to feel just right. The process is more art than science: no market studies, no focus groups. Only living the lifestyle. Because to create a strong lifestyle brand, you have to live the life. And that's the requirement of every designer on the in-house team. Pottery Barn wants to create inspiration, so the input must reflect vitality. Designers go to popular eateries and watering holes to see how tables are set. They pick through flea markets for the one-of-a-kind finds. They go dreaming by visiting new model homes and dropping in on real estate open houses. They're encouraged to entertain often and record wish-list items.

All fodder for brainstorming, the collected ideas and input make their way to the Inspiration Room, where they get bundled, sorted, and categorized. As themes emerge from the various finds, storyboards and palettes are created. Once a potential new product passes muster on compulsory quality and durability, it must then pass a strict three-point test centered on the softer side of things.

1. Looks great—The item has to be aesthetically pleasing to the eye. But it can't be out on the lunatic fringe, too cutting edge. Design standards call for every product to be directionally out front, but in an abundant way. Meaning everyone can relate to it.

2. Feels good—The product has to tingle the touch, to comfort and caress. Rough fabrics and coarse materials don't make the cut.

3. Fits perfectly—The ultimate test is a simple question to the staffers: Would you take it home or give it as a present to your best friend? The slightest hesitation and the item goes back to the drawing board or gets the heave-ho.

At Pottery Barn, emotion is engineered into every product.

The Gallup Organization includes a measure of love in the eleven questions making up its "Customer Engagement" survey: "I can't imagine a world without [company or brand]."

The following stories about the stuff we love offer some insight into the world of intangible value. They demonstrate the fact that people are buying something more than the product or service. They prove the power of intangibles to differentiate and distinguish. Here's a hint: Look for the emotional or perceptual aspect.

Prius

When we hear the word "engineer," we immediately think "rational." But you'd think just the opposite in listening to Toyota chief engineer Masao Inoue talk about the popular hybrid Prius, as he's quoted in *Lovemarks* by Kevin Roberts:

"The feel of a car often comes down to the small things, like the feel when you actually touch the material, leather, or wood. This is a new kind of thinking, thinking of how things feel to the consumer. To make my decisions, I must always ride in the car. There are many things that you cannot find from data that you discover when you ride in a car. There is nothing, no machine, that can replace the human body. It is the best sensor. For example, when you turn the steering wheel, sometimes you can just feel a sound. So faint you can't really measure it, but the feel of it is there. Also, things like the glove box, the console box, or the cup holder. When you open and close them they create their own sounds. And there are often faint sounds that can really irritate the person who is driving a car. The aim is to create a stillness that you can't actually measure by figures in the normal sense, and this is done by feeling and touch.

"With the Prius we talk about quietness. Now noise can be measured by figures, but there is also a quietness that you feel with your body. For instance, with regard to the acceleration, the Prius is very different from other cars. You can time the speed of acceleration with a stopwatch, but the actual speed and the body's perception of it are very different. Of course, we do measure these things, and we set some target figures. But just because we get the target figure we're after, it doesn't mean it's okay.

Figures are figures. We need to be able to feel the quietness or feel good about the acceleration as we actually experience it in the car. I think these things are very important."

Apple Computer

Everyone knows that Apple Computer is synonymous with design. But not everyone knows that what's driving that design is the notion that Apple customers are making a statement in buying an Apple product. They're making society know that they have good taste, that they're daring to "Think Different" from the conventional electronics crowd. It is of little or no consequence that a competing product to an iMac, iPod, or PowerBook is cheaper or faster or has more features. Apple's design is not a branding gimmick; it's part of the company's heritage, dating back to the 1970s' desire of Steve Jobs to make the Apple II an aesthetically appealing, house-friendly personal computer.

JetBlue

JetBlue CEO David Neeleman knows how to deliver the personal touch, beyond the low fares, leather seats, satellite TV, and on-time arrivals. He knows his employees by name, knows their family. He's fond of walking down the aisles of one of his twin-engine Airbus A320 aircrafts, meeting and greeting, chatting and collecting business cards, asking for input and jotting down suggestions from customers. Or serving. Or cleaning up after landing. He works weekly alongside the flight crew, helping them create "the JetBlue experience." Says Neeleman: *"Not everything resonates with every customer. Some people like the leather seats, some like the TV, some like the fact that we don't overbook our flights. I don't care if they don't notice everything we do. Just as long as they notice something that's different about us."*

> *Every new product or service that Virgin Group offers must have the best quality, provide great value, be innovative, dramatically challenge existing alternatives, and provide a "sense of fun" or "cheekiness."*
> **Richard Branson**

Lexus

Lexus takes intangibles very seriously. There's probably nothing more intangible than perfection, which it pursues with passion. J. Davis Illingworth, former Lexus Division general manager, recalls an early story of intangible perfection:

> *"At one point on a visit to Japan in 1987, I spent an entire day with Lexus chief engineer Shoji Jimbo. Only then did I gain a real appreciation of the incredible thoroughness with which Jimbo and his team approached the creation of the LS400. At one point we were talking about the key. There's a very special look and shape and feel to the Lexus key. Jimbo excused himself from our discussion, went into his office, and returned with a box. He opened the box and dumped the contents out on the table. He said that the box contained the keys from every car in the world. Then Jimbo held up the Lexus key and proudly said, 'We have studied every car key in the world. This is the best key in the world for the best car in the world!'"*

> What we sell is the ability for a 43-year old accountant to dress in black leather, ride through small towns and have people be afraid of him.
> **Harley-Davidson executive**

Studio D

Outside Chicago, people take a two-hour round-trip excursion to shop and learn at a stylish electronics retailer known as Studio D. Once there, they can relax, browse at their leisure, and take classes in digital media, photography, and software. The cozy setting, inviting nooks, and warm decor provide a welcome change from the big-box stores like Best Buy. Who's behind the concept? Why, Best Buy, naturally. The idea is an experiment in catering to the druthers of Best Buy's best customers: young, hip, high-tech adults.

Best Buy has another concept store in the works, called Escape. While Studio D is all about warmth, Escape is all about chrome and polish, with a nightclub feel. The goal for both is to deliver a mood and create a community-centric retail experience closely connected to the residential surroundings. The expectation is that buyers will visit the shop as much to meet up with a friend as to browse the product offerings. The personal touch is accomplished through club-type memberships providing tailored services such as individual consultations, access to private parties, custom graphics services, and outings to local sports events. Executives hold high hopes that customers will network and eventually become loyal evangelists, a kind of extended sales force. The customer reaction is right on the mark: "I love this store!"

Anthropologie

Anthropologie customers are passionate about the store. Not because of the apparel, accessories, and furnishings. Because of what it inspires: a sense of originality, an adventure of self-discovery. In other words, the experience. It's a crossroads of commerce and culture.

When you walk into an Anthropologie, you walk into another world. Rather, worlds. Italy, France, Morocco, the Far East. It's all there for you to experience. Handcrafted, one-of-a-kind furniture pieces act as elegant clothing racks for an eclectic ensemble of garments ranging from vintage to fashion-forward. Laced pillows, embroidered throw rugs, copper urns, leather-bound books, wrought iron tables, old baskets, all somehow blend together in an uncanny array of uniqueness.

There must be a method to the madness, but it isn't visible. Zero categories. More like small vignettes adorning a winding path. Somehow every emotion, every sense is magically activated through the density and dynamism of the merchandising. It's a vibrant space that sets a distinct mood and creates a compelling context. Everything is named, and everything has a story. President Glen Shenk puts it this way: *"Our focus is on always doing what's right for a specific customer we know very well. Our customers are our friends, and what we do is never, ever, ever about selling to them."*

Such is the art of the intangible.

FYI

Intangibles figure into the calculation of the monthly Consumer Price Index (CPI). The CPI applies the principles of hedonics.

Hedonics is a way of taking into account product improvements when tracking price movement. In other words, a $600 computer this month won't be a $600 computer next month, even if the price stays the same. It may be less if a new model selling at the same price comes out offering improvement over the current model.

The term itself means "the doctrine of pleasure," and was adopted by General Motors economist Andrew Court in the 1930s when searching for a name for his statistical method emphasizing the link over time between car prices, consumer utility, and automotive features.

ToolKit: Targeting the Intangibles

Security comes in many forms. Some are secure in the knowledge that an experience will be fun. Some are secure knowing others will approve. Personal touch is all about the personal definition of security. It's about what matters most.

Scan the words below, all of which are different ways people have described security. Which might represent an intangible level of value for your products and services? Which might represent something your competitors offer that you don't?

Acceptance	Deference	Individuality	Reality
Adventure	Dependability	Immediacy	Recognition
Affection	Discipline	Impulse	Refuge
Affiliation	Energy	Inclusion	Renewal
Action	Equality	Integrity	Respectability
Approval	Esteem	Intelligence	Ritual
Attention	Elegance	Intimacy	Routine
Authenticity	Excitement	Joy	Safety
Authority	Escape	Kinship	Sanctuary
Autonomy	Exclusivity	Leadership	Self-discovery
Balance	Expertise	Longevity	Self-expression
Beauty	Fame	Magic	Self-reliance
Belonging	Family	Mystery	Sensitivity
Brotherhood	Fantasy	Novelty	Serenity
Calm	Freedom	Opportunity	Simplicity
Camaraderie	Friendship	Order	Spirituality
Caring	Fun	Partnership	Spontaneity
Certainty	Goodwill	Passion	Solitude
Challenge	Grace	Peace of mind	Stability
Comfort	Harmony	Personality	Status
Commitment	Heritage	Play	Stimulation
Community	Health	Pleasure	Tranquillity
Competition	Honesty	Popularity	Understanding
Conformity	Honor	Power	Unity
Connection	Hope	Predictability	Variety
Control	Humor	Prestige	Vitality
Credibility	Image	Pride	Well-being
Culture	Identity	Procedure	Wisdom
Daring	Independence	Quiet	Wonder

MORE THAN A FEELING

One of the most powerful intangibles relates to the idea of *partnership*; that is, a mutually beneficial exchange of value in which each partner is essentially helping the other succeed. A collaboration. A feeling of *we're in this together.*

Most of us have had some horrible consumer experience that left us cold. Yet we stayed with the provider. In fact, we may have even deepened our relationship. Our trust in them actually grew. Why? Because they stepped up, righted their wrong and *demonstrated caring.* Caring is a surefire security blanket. When we weather a hardship with a partner, we emerge stronger.

Lexus experienced just such an effect inside three months after the maiden launch of the LS400 in 1989. A faulty activator switch in the cruise control system caused the overdrive to kick in.

The swift action taken was, and remains, unprecedented. Lexus replaced the part on every LS400, not wasting any time determining which cars had bad parts. The recall had the potential to devastate the Lexus image. Critics snickered over the "Relentless Pursuit of Perfection." They underestimated the creativity and resolve of Lexus, which mobilized the entire organization on both sides of the Pacific. Toyota provided parts in record time from Japan. Senior Toyota executives sent video messages by satellite to dealers. Lexus corporate and regional managers called on dealers to personally deliver the details.

The response by the dealers made it all work. They moved Lexus from being a question mark in consumers' minds to being the industry benchmark for customer care. At no cost to owners, cars were picked up by the dealer, repaired and returned promptly—washed and with a full tank of gas. In less than three weeks, 8,000 vehicles were repaired, tested and returned to their owners, in time for Christmas.

The honesty, speed, and efficiency in handling the recall buttressed the brand as one of trust. It was a defining moment proving that Lexus was everything it had been promised to be.

And perfectly intangible.

Hansei

What intangible value do you provide customers?

What distinguishes you from your competition?

What are your customers really purchasing?

What one word would customers use to describe your company?

How do internal and external perceptions match up?

CHAPTER 9

Leverage the Limits

Art consists of limitation. The most beautiful part of every picture is the frame.

G. K. Chesterton

Restraining Forces Rule—Resource Constraints Can Spur Ingenuity

Problem: *The entrepreneurial spirit is M.I.A.* We're stuck. Stuck in the old school, stuck in the status quo, stuck in stall. We want things done differently, but we can't seem to get there from here. We've lost our edge. The days of rapid innovation are disappearing in the rearview mirror, replaced by rapidly approaching competition. There's widespread lethargy. The one word that strikes fear in the heart of leaders and managers everywhere looms large: *complacency.*

Cause: *Addiction to abundant resources.* "We need more money, people, and space to innovate." But that's not how you started. Somewhere in your company tree is a story not unlike Toyota's humble beginnings. Maybe you didn't start in the attic or garage, but you started with little of everything: money, space, labor. You had a goal, and a passion for reaching it. Those limits made you more creative and resourceful than you are today. Today, the addiction to resources is blocking innovation.

Solution: *Reset the bar.* Get back to the future. Get the band back together. Get back to basics. Get back to blocking and tackling. Return to your roots. And all the other clichés that spring to mind for vanquishing the complacency that comes with success. To recapture the start-up spirit, re-create the kinds of limitations that drive new thinking.

Then trust your team to solve the problem.

CREATIVE CHAINS

No one was shocked when Toyota president Katsuaki Watanabe announced to Wall Street and the world in the latter part of 2005 that he had ordered his research chief Masatami Takimoto to find a way to cut in half the $5,000 price difference between Toyota's hybrid cars and similar gasoline models, without compromising any of the current quality standards, features, and performance.

> *My goal is to reduce that difference to one-half the current levels...I assume Mr. Takimoto must be racking his brains about how to do that.*
> **Katsuaki Watanabe**
> President, Toyota

That's the Toyota way. Since World War II, resource constraints have been a key driver of innovation at Toyota.

Toyota treats resource constraints the same way artists do. All artists work within the confines of their chosen media, and it's the limits that spur their creativity. The canvas edge, the marble block, the eight musical notes—the resources are finite. They always *are*—restraining forces *always* rule! So it's how you view and manage them that makes all the difference. And that's the $64 million question: *Are limits preventing innovation, or enabling it?*

There's only one right answer. A team that doesn't thrive on the challenge of limitations is a red flag. It means there is an inherent fear of failure in your organization. And that spells danger for innovation, because most real innovation springs from failure and conflict. And most organizations have little tolerance for either. So they mismanage a valuable source of new thinking by adding a buffer zone: higher budgets, more layers, and lower expectations.

> *In these days, a man who says a thing cannot be done is quite apt to be interrupted by some idiot doing it.*
> **Elbert Green Hubbard**

Success rarely breeds the kind of thinking that produces the extraordinary results needed to add value and keep competitors at bay. It generates a defensive posture that discourages the very behavior that created it. It can absolutely stifle innovation.

Innovation demands exploiting limits, not ignoring them.

Mission Impossible

Exploiting Limitations Drives Breakthrough Thinking

Santa Monica Freeway

The January 1994 Northridge, California earthquake devastated the Santa Monica Freeway, leaving 350,000 daily commuters no access to L.A. Early estimates predicted at least 12 months to rebuild, at a public cost of $1 million for each day the freeway was shut down.

Innovative constructor C. C. Myers saw it differently. He saw it as a 4.5-month project. Staking his wealth and reputation, C. C. Myers signed a $14.7 million contract with the city, which allowed a maximum completion time of 140 calendar days, with a penalty for late completion of $205,000 per calendar day and an incentive of $200,000 per day for early completion and opening the freeway to traffic.

Mission: *Impossible.*

Approach: *Change everything.*

Results: *Spectacular.*

Contract time commenced on February 5 with materials and equipment moving to the jobsite that same day and through the weekend, even though final construction plans were not available until February 26. C. C. Myers immediately went to work on a 24/7 schedule with up to 400 workmen on the job. On-site inspectors were used to eliminate delay and rework. Workers were running on the job. Special quick-setting concrete was used. Subcontract bids and awards were made on a daily basis. Work flowed.

Sixty-six days after the contract was signed, the Santa Monica Freeway was opened to traffic, 74 days ahead of schedule.

ToolKit: Stretch Goals

The Lexus story illustrates the ability of Toyota to stretch its prowess in design, engineering and production. The Scion story illustrates the stretch of the imagination. There will be other "stretch" stories to follow.

Stretch goals are a prime tool for innovation. Artfully set, they define the limits that spur ingenuity. Jim Collins refers to stretch goals as "BHAGs" in his 1994 book *Built to Last*—Big, Hairy, Audacious Goals that represent ambitious plans intended to fire up the whole company. He's right. Done right, they work.

One of the most relevant and compelling examples of how stretch goals can transform ordinary thinking is the story of Toyota's North American Parts Operation (NAPO), which in 2000 launched what it called, appropriately enough, "Stretch Goals." NAPO is the parts and accessories distribution arm of Toyota Motor Sales, U.S.A. Inc., and is responsible for serving over 1200 Toyota, Lexus, and Scion dealers and distributors in North America, Mexico, Puerto Rico, Hawaii, and Micronesia. A $2.7 billion business, NAPO is home to nearly 1700 employees operating two major stocking facilities and eleven distribution centers.

Here's what happened.

In the early part of 2000, Toyota's service parts and accessories business was booming. But times weren't all that good at NAPO. They had just come off a difficult expansion effort, moving from a domestic procurement operation essentially dedicated to Japan to a global supply chain sourcing parts from 600 different suppliers around the world. Launch of the second of two major parts stocking hubs was coming up in 18 months. A change in senior management was made, which added another dimension to an organization in transition.

Jane Beseda, newly appointed vice president and general manager, one of Toyota's most successful senior executives, had a goal of adding compelling value, of making a difference to the organization and to customers worldwide.

Upon her arrival, she saw a benchmark parts operation able to fill 98% of its dealer orders within 24 hours; no easy feat with 20 million Toyotas on the road. She saw a sophisticated supply chain with rising *costs and increasingly high customer requirements in spite of the new facilities and added capability meant to do just the opposite. She saw warehouse capacity being strained by over three months' supply of inventory worth over $350 million, made up of over 200,000 parts numbers for nearly 30 Toyota models. She saw the effects of global coverage through local production—procuring and supplying global distributors in radically different markets with widely varying regulations was difficult to manage well.*

She stands back to appraise an enormously complex organization run by tremendously talented people…who aren't working together as well as she thinks they can. She has a dream. She wants three things, and she wants them simultaneously:

1. *$100 million in distribution cost savings*
2. *$100 million of inventory removed from the supply chain*
3. *50% improvement in customer service*

Jane didn't know the parts business, but she didn't need to. She knew business, people, and organizations. She knew how to manage and motivate. She knew the program would foster transformation by forcing collaboration, cooperation, and communication across functional silos. The goals simply couldn't be met otherwise. She knew she couldn't dictate solutions. But she knew that a new structure and system for planning was required, one that let the ideas spring up and take root.

Still, her staff was slightly stunned, because the targets were three-year goals! Three years was the right timeline, the perfect stretch. It's enough time to move the needle. Less than three was entirely impossible, demotivating. More than three and the vision was too distant, disengaging.

Jane named her effort Stretch Goals. The focus would be bilateral: externally on customers, internally on costs. There would be no more business as usual, and the bar got set high:

1. *Reduce inventory*   *50%*
2. *Increase throughput*   *25%*
3. *Reduce freight costs*   *25%*
4. *Reduce packaging expense* *50%*

5. *Increase space utilization*   25%

6. *Decrease back orders*   50%

7. *Improve safety/decrease errors* 50%

8. *Decrease lead time*   40%

9. *Reduce damage*   50%

10. *Decrease landfill usage*   25%

The goals were simple, memorable. No fancy mission statements or paralyzing wordsmithing needed. This was supply-chain transformation, clear and simple.

The goals were superstretch, almost unreachable. Almost but not quite. Counterintuitive, yes. But Jane knew that a 10% improvement could be more difficult to achieve than a 50% improvement, because a 10% improvement almost always translates into working harder, not smarter. Fifty percent improvement simply cannot be achieved by logging overtime. Tactical tweaks wouldn't cut it either.

The goals would send the right message: Think differently and extend your reach beyond your grasp. They would serve to inspire and motivate, energize and engage. They would stimulate progress like never before. But it would have to be all hands on deck.

The first step was to set up a command central function to manage the whole process. Not direct it, but support it. Jane called on Strategic Planning Manager Thor Oxnard to set up a Project Management Office. Thor dug a new job: making the PMO a key strategic move designed to provide central coordination and monitoring of progress toward the targets. Done right, it would result in better project integration, planning, and cross-organizational communication.

The next step was to move beyond concept. It was time for action, prioritization, and measurement. The targets had to be data-based and verifiable. Savings had to drop to the bottom line. Soft numbers wouldn't work. Reality crept in; the effort had to be transparent, open-book. The targets were aligned to the business, sure, but everyone involved would have to be in tune with the finances if the effort was going to have a shot at working. They would need to see what executives see. Sharing general ledger items like business-line profitability with associates was unheard of. But innovative.

Next it was time to communicate and enlist. Eighty top managers flew in to NAPO headquarters to hear Jane introduce Stretch Goals. Heads spun a bit. There was dissonance, but then, there had to be. There would be no movement without it. It seemed that there were too many targets, all at once. There was no clear direction, no specific orders. Breakout sessions were used to develop high-level initiatives addressing each target.

The key task for each manager would be: "Return to your respective facility and think through your ideas. Call on your supervisors and associates. We meet again in two months." No marching orders, just ideas.

In January 2001, the management team huddled again. This time they were fired up, chanting "$100 million, we can do it!" Ideas were prioritized, action items created and assigned. Things began to gel. A project agenda emerged, representing a unified approach. Suddenly saving $100 million in three years seemed somehow reachable. Key performance indicators for each target were developed and agreed to.

For example, damage reduction would be measured as pieces per million shipped and damage dollars as a percentage of sales. Baselines were set using year 2000 results. Finally, the PMO was introduced as the mechanism to track and coordinate all; Thor's concept hit the mark and the PMO was well received. NAPO vice president Fletcher Davidson promised to do cartwheels if the targets were met.

By June 2001, some progress was being made. But something was missing. Changes were still functional. The cross-organizational projects hadn't materialized as hoped.

Realization dawned that the only way innovation in operating processes would occur with enough impact to achieve Stretch Goal targets would be through execution of cross-organizational projects. But project teams were struggling to coordinate work in the traditional functional department planning approach. Systems thinking would be required to consider potential impact of plans on other functions and areas of the broader organization. A better mechanism would be needed to ensure projects had mutual support as well as PMO support.

Solution: create midrange plans using a Vertical-Horizontal-Vertical (V-H-V) planning process, involving three steps:

- **Vertical**—*Each department would plan as it normally does within its functional silo.*

- **Horizontal**—*Representatives from each department would then gather to discuss and coordinate their plans in order to identify impacts on other areas and to request support.*

- **Vertical**—*Local plans would be updated with new information based on other department actions, then published and circulated.*

The V-H-V structure changed the culture. At one level, the organization became more adept at planning—listening to one another, communicating, respecting other ideas, and developing much more cohesive teams. At another level, NAPO started having fun. V-H-V meetings ended in laughter, demonstrating the camaraderie. Year-end celebrations were held with all associates at all locations to present achievements, with managers serving breakfast in chef hats.

The scene in November 2003 is euphoric: a hotel conference room in Southern California filled to capacity, with an announcer's voice saying over the PA, "Three years ago NAPO was given a challenge they said couldn't be done." Lights flash as Jane Beseda and her leadership team run through the crowd in true pro basketball fashion. The crowd is chanting, "Fletcher!" Fletcher appears ready to cartwheel. Pink Floyd's "Money" is booming as Jane pulls a cord to unfurl a banner reading **"Thanks a $100 Million"** *and play money $100 million bills float down like confetti. On each is Fletcher Davidson doing a cartwheel.*

Victory!

Leveraging the limits, 101.

Stretching on the Front Line

NAPO's Stretch Goals Spur Everyday Ingenuity

Thinking about the Box

Things get a little complex when thirteen parts facilities use their own local packing material vendor to supply parts overpack boxes. Such was the case at NAPO. 156 different box sizes were being utilized to ship the same parts. Local purchasing of boxes had resulted in nearly $23 million of overpack costs.

Then came Stretch Goals, with the goal of reducing packaging costs up to 50% and ultimately moving to standardized box sizes centrally sourced through a single national supplier.

To get everyone involved, the Packaging Reduction Team first held interfacility meetings conducted via videoconferencing in order to grasp the situation and gain insight into the problem. Representatives from each parts facility participated and gave input. Meeting facilitation was no easy feat, but eventually the group began working as a team.

To understand why packaging costs were so high, lists of suppliers and materials from each center were gathered and analyzed. The team discovered significant variation in box sizes, with a lot of customization.

Next, the team came to consensus on standard box sizes, with the original 156 being reduced to 18 sizes that made sense. Once that was decided, the task of coordinating integration of the new sizes into the operation began.

The third phase entailed reducing the number of materials vendors to a single national supplier.

The result: savings of over $10 million in three years!

STRETCH GOAL SETTING

Not all of NAPO's targets were met. But close enough: $100 million in cost savings, $90 million taken out of inventory, and 35% improvement in customer service. A few lessons emerge from the NAPO Stretch Goals story. They're embedded in the case itself, but are worth highlighting. A well-set stretch goal is four things:

1. Aligned. Properly set goals can be transformational if they're tied closely to what is most important to the organization. In NAPO's case, all goals clearly linked to the Toyota core values of continuous improvement and respect for people, and to NAPO's mission: *To provide world-class parts suppliability at the lowest cost.*

2. Audacious. Committing to a compelling set of daunting stretch goals is a powerful way to stimulate innovation while achieving extraordinary business results. Stretch goals are a breed apart. They can't be achieved easily or quickly. Set well, they're a rallying point and provide energy and focus that perhaps wasn't there before.

3. Articulate. "Fifty percent safety improvement" is a clear target. It's real. It's not in any way a fanciful statement disconnected to the business. It's easy to grasp, and everyone gets it right away. A well-set goal stands alone without need of further explanation, not unlike Kennedy's 1961 mission to land on the moon by the end of the decade.

4. Arduous. Easy goals don't require innovation. A good stretch goal is one that is achievable, but only through innovative thinking, real struggle, and a dash of luck. If it's too hard, though—truly impossible—people will disengage from the process entirely.

Exploiting the limits through stretch goals is an art in itself!

Exercise: The Power of Stretch

What would you attempt if you knew you couldn't fail?

It's a trick question, because you can't fail in the *attempt*, only in the *outcome*. When the goal itself is to try, there's no failure. It's just that the test comes before the lesson. Think of the best mistake you ever made, an instance when everyone told you not to do something, but you did it anyway. Now think of the biggest risk you ever took. Now think of your most powerful learning experience. Unless I miss my guess, they all involve the same event.

If you forever indulge in the fear of failure, you'll never experience the heights of your power. Our greatest growth occurs when we take intelligent risks and push the limits. We often surprise ourselves when we step outside our comfort zone and rise to a new challenge.

> *The first and greatest victory is to conquer yourself; to be conquered by yourself is of all things most shameful and vile.*
> **Plato**

Here's the thing: Most of our limitations are self-imposed. To quickly illustrate the point, try this exercise.

1. *Stand up, feet planted shoulder width apart, arms straight out at your sides, elbows locked.*

2. *Twist your torso all the way to the right as far as you possibly can go.*

3. *Sight down your right arm and mentally mark your stopping point on the wall. Remember that mark.*

4. *Turn back around to face front. Now close your eyes.*

5. *Repeat the exercise, stopping when you think you've met your previous stopping point.*

6. *NOW...go a little past it. Open your eyes.*

My bet is that you surpassed your previous mark. Point being, we generally don't know what our potential is until we put our capacity on trial.

Structural Hazards

Many of the cases covered so far point out the organizational need for new structures and systems to accommodate big innovative efforts that result in essentially new business ventures. At Toyota, for example, Lexus and Scion are separate divisions within the larger organization. They have different distribution schemes and different dealership agreements, separate and distinct from the Toyota brand. NAPO Stretch Goals required a new structure, the Project Management Office.

But beware of putting the cart before the horse. You don't need a new structure or system if you don't have a real idea or innovation. In fact, it can backfire on you if you're not careful.

It happened at Toyota. It was called Genesis, and it was a star-crossed attempt to attract Gen Y consumers, kids of baby boomers, to the Toyota brand. Toyota set up Genesis as a separate strategic marketing team. The idea was to reposition the Toyota brand through hip new imagery and advertising dreamed up by a younger, supposedly edgier team of professionals. Toyota committed millions of dollars, but no new products. The assumption was that the existing lineup would work. No such luck. Genesis disbanded in February 2000, a dismal failure.

> *Because its purpose is to create a customer, the business enterprise has two— and only these two—basic functions: marketing and innovation.*
> **Peter Drucker**

Recall Peter Drucker's stance that business gets down to two essential functions: innovation and marketing. If you only have half the game— marketing only, in the case of Genesis—you don't need a new structure. You need the *innovation*.

Yet out of the Genesis failure came the overwhelming success of Scion. As is the Toyota way, the learning from failure gave rise to innovation.

So it should be with your company.

HANSEI

What's holding you back?

How can you reframe current limitations?

How do you view risk and failure?

When was the last time you celebrated a flop?

Which of your goals will stimulate new thinking?

CHAPTER 10

Master the Tension

No problem can withstand the assault of sustained thinking.
Voltaire

Breakthrough Thinking Demands Something to Break Through

Problem: *Solutions lack inspiration.* And imagination, originality. We don't think as deeply or as broadly as we must to solve the problem. We throw some resources at the problem and move on. Or tweak a previous solution and fit it to the current situation. Or alter the situation to fit our solution, usually by lowering the goal or target, instead of pressing the issue and hanging in there until we've exhausted our best thinking. We favor implementation over incubation. Then we wonder why the reaction to our idea is ho-hum.

Cause: *We satisfice.* Satisfy plus suffice, which is to say *good enough.* It's a term economist and Nobel Laureate Herbert A. Simon coined in his 1957 *Models of Man* to describe the typical human decision-making process by which we go with the first option that offers an acceptable payoff. We'll take whatever seems to meet the bare minimum requirement to achieve the goal. Then we stop looking for the best way to solve the problem. That flies in the face of ingenuity and the pursuit of perfection. In the end, it's selfish, because the customer loses.

Solution: *Work through creative tension.* Make its resolution mandatory. Stay the course to meet all goals. Pair goals to conflict with others to prevent compromise and dilution. Breakthrough thinking comes from breaking through the mental barrier erected by the obvious solutions.

THE SPACE BETWEEN

Great innovation is often born of an ability to harmonize opposing tensions. Like the pressure to avoid failure and the need to take risks. Or the demands of getting results quickly and the freedom to search for the best way. Unfortunately, we have a natural tendency to give in too early and grab the easy solution that is inevitably less than elegant, less than optimal.

Many of the world's most compelling works of art use the theme of tension between opposites to create an aura of ambiguity and uncertainty. That's what draws our attention. It's not what's actually there on the canvas, it's what *may or may not* be there that we find so fascinating. Artists favor the implied over the blatant, the hint over the obvious. Musicians use the silence between notes to create the dramatic tension that makes the piece powerful. Sculptors are as sensitive to the space surrounding their art as they are to the work itself.

In much the same way, the spaces between your definitive actions and firm decisions can hold the key to elegant problem solving. This much is true: as the pace of change accelerates and complexity grows, certainty fades while ambiguity multiplies.

How well you're able to handle the space between where you are and where you want to be has everything to do with how well you solve problems and how successful you are at innovation.

ToolKit: Dynamic Tension

One of the most powerful tools in this book, and in Toyota's repertoire, is this one: *Dynamic Tension*. Dynamic Tension is a term coined here for a strategic mechanism that spurs breakthrough thinking. It's the setting of opposing forces in

Perspective

Leonardo da Vinci was a great believer in using tension between opposites to create intrigue through the effects of uncertainty and ambiguity.

Da Vinci's *Mona Lisa* is the ultimate expression of paradox. Her mysterious half-smile has been interpreted as the opposition of good and evil, compassion and cruelty, and seduction and innocence. The corners of her eyes and mouth are left ambiguous and open to interpretation. The general haziness about the entire work leaves something to the imagination.

Virgin of the Rocks employs a central theme of opposition and contrast. The tranquillity of the almost smiling angel and the mother with children is surrounded by a manic background suggesting the end of the world.

direct competition or conflict with each other, purposefully creating a Dynamic Tension that demands harmonious resolution.

Dynamic Tension eliminates the tendency to satisfice by making it impossible to succeed without thinking differently. It's the corollary to the technique discussed in the previous chapter of using constraints to drive change and innovation.

Dynamic Tension can be employed in a number of ways. Here's how.

Lexus 2

Let's return to the story of the Lexus LS400 from Chapter 2. Chief Engineer Suzuki set the bar high to beat, not match, Mercedes and BMW: The Lexus would have a top speed of 155 mph, fuel efficiency over 22.5 mpg, a drag of .29, and a noise level of 58 dB at 60 mph, and a curb weight of 3800 pounds. The ride itself had to be smoother and more stable, with better handling at higher speeds. It had to be a more pleasant driving experience. The styling had to be elegant and refined.

But it wasn't simply that designers and engineers were attempting to beat the best across the board. It's that almost all of the targets conflicted with each other. Almost all the engineers and designers thought the task was impossible. The individual targets were individually attainable, although each a stretch. But taken together? Impossible.

Greater speed and acceleration conflicts directly with fuel efficiency, noise, and weight, because higher speed and acceleration requires a more powerful engine. A more powerful engine is a bigger and heavier engine, so it makes more noise and consumes more fuel. A smooth, quiet ride conflicts directly with lower weight and better handling at high speed. Heavy, non-performance-oriented cars with beefier insulation and softer suspension provide the smoother, more quiet ride. Refined styling and high-speed stability conflicts directly with aerodynamic drag. At the time, elegance in styling wasn't the streamlined look it is today. Too, the more angled look of luxury passenger cars provided greater stability due to the higher air friction.

The resulting success of the Lexus LS400 was due in large part to the Dynamic Tension between all the various competing targets, combined with Chief Engineer Suzuki's refusal to compromise, to hold and master the tension.

The technique was used in subsequent LS product planning. In developing the next generation LS, product planners at Toyota Motor Sales asked the chief engineer for three things: faster 0 to 60 acceleration, better fuel efficiency, and greater silence. The only way to achieve all three was to find ways to take weight out of the vehicle. In the end, some 60 kilograms (over 120 pounds) were eliminated. The goal was accomplished, as one manager tells the story, *"gram by gram."*

For another example, let's return to the NAPO Stretch Goals story in the previous chapter.

NAPO 2

Toyota's NAPO headquarters saw the ultimate mission of the Stretch Goals initiative as optimizing the entire supply chain. But attempting to do that simply by issuing some big, aggressive goals ignores the nuance of the system, irrespective of how well intentioned or well aligned they may be. There are inherent conflicts existing between and among the various natural functions of any supply chain. The real beauty of NAPO's strategy was in recognizing those tensions, calling attention to them, and capitalizing on them to power new thinking and drive cross-group collaboration.

Recall the ten stretches? To the casual observer this seems like a simple master wish list. But look closer. See if you can spot the tension points.

1. Reduce inventory   50%
2. Increase throughput   25%
3. Reduce freight costs   25%
4. Reduce packaging expense   50%
5. Increase space utilization   25%
6. Decrease back orders   50%
7. Improve safety/decrease errors 50%
8. Decrease lead time   40%
9. Reduce damage   50%
10. Decrease landfill usage   25%

Here's a hint. Take a look at inventory and back orders, stretch goals #1 and #6 in the list above. In most supply chains, they're opposite sides of the same coin. Increase inventory, and back orders drop. Decrease it, and back orders generally rise. So NAPO brilliantly, and counterintuitively, paired the two, pitting one against the other to create the Dynamic Tension. Take a look at how all ten goals were paired.

Inventory Reduction (-50%) v. Back Orders (-50%)	Packaging Expense (-50%) v. Damage (-50%)	Throughput (+25%) v. Errors/Safety (-50%)	Space Utilization (+25%) v. Landfill (-25%)	Freight Costs (-25%) v. Lead Time (-40%)

One more case describes Dynamic Tension on a macro level.

Prius & the Birth of Toyota's Competitive Design Strategy

For at least a decade Toyota has employed a unique internal design process few other companies attempt, either because they haven't thought of it, or because they'd rather look outside the organization for innovation.

Toyota's three major design locations—Tokyo, California, and Europe—compete to design every new model. Awards are made based on the best and most innovative new design. That way, what keeps most senior executives up at night—complacency in an increasingly design-centric marketplace—is less a threat at Toyota than elsewhere.

It all began with the design of Toyota's best-selling hybrid Prius.

In 1995, Chief Engineer Takeshi Uchiyamada wasn't all that enamored of the various designs submitted for the production model Prius. They weren't living up to the name, which meant "before" in Latin, indicating before the twenty-first century. They weren't much better than the overly sensational concept designed by the Head Office Advanced Design Team and displayed that year in the Tokyo Auto Show. They were either too conservative or too eccentric. They were either too Corolla-like, or too concept-car-like. They didn't capture the essence of the new hybrid system and the new era dawning.

As it always is in Toyota, compromise was not an option. Uchiyamada promised to wait for the arrival of the perfect design, stating, "We will not give up and say that something is good enough." He then contacted headquarters and requested an organized competition between all of the design divisions. Seven teams would compete: Head Office Design, Tokyo Design Division, Vehicle Development Division II, a contract design team at Toyota, Toyoda Automatic Loom Works Design Division, Toyota's CALTY of California, and Toyota's European Office of Creation (EPOC) in Brussels. All were to submit designs.

Uchiyamada went so far as to urge Toyota's board to allow entry from outside design studios such as Italy's Carrozeria. The idea was squashed for purposes of secrecy. Initially disappointed, Uchiyamada would later say, "Having completed such a difficult design within the company, Toyota's design division gained a lot of confidence. It was definitely a good thing we did it internally."

The competition worked, stimulating wide-ranging creativity. More than 20 sketches were submitted, all innovative. Initial judging focused on defining the range. Uchiyamada was surprised at the breadth of ideas, given an identical set of starting assumptions. EOC's designs were typically European: two-box (passenger, engine, no trunk). Japan's designs were typically Japanese: three-box (passenger, engine, trunk). CALTY's submission attracted the most attention: egg-shaped but three-box. Designer Irwin Lui had created a form by slowly applying pressure from the two ends of a hard-boiled egg until it almost fell apart, and captured the shape. The result was a three-box design with a monoform profile.

Five designs were selected, and the designers invited to submit clay models. Four were submitted, and two were exceptional: CALTY's and that of the Head Office Design. Both had drawbacks. CALTY's violated the requirement of a three-box sedan: It appeared to have a trunk, but was in fact a five-door hatchback. CALTY had decided to risk the violation in favor of a stronger, more progressive design. The Head Office package was unique and conceptually coherent, but lacked the feel of the future.

By May 1996, there was no decision. A semifinal review round was to be made in the summer. It would be a panel review, with several hundred panelists chosen from nontechnology departments. Scoring would be based on two dozen criteria. The winning design would become official upon approval from Toyota's president and board. Final review would be the design award.

Irwin Lui traveled to Japan to make certain refinements, sculpting a final look. He introduced new, sweeping lines above the wheel arches to give it a fresh look. He would be heard to say that he was treating the body like a painter's canvas, using subtle surface curves devoid of hard detail. The design split the audience into two distinct camps: They either loved it or hated it.

The competition was in full heat. Uchiyamada thought the CALTY design would be too hard to produce. Anticipating a Head Office victory, he began noodling with the design details.

Anxiety was running high at the final review in July 1996. The final Head Office design was definitely a new direction, but conservative. The CALTY design was something foreign to Toyota. Both designs went far beyond the 1995 concept car. Both were truly innovative.

Board members were split. But the final decision would rest with the panel. The results were close. Very close. But clear. CALTY's design won in every category: futurity, innovation, female, and youth appeal.

Uchiyamada's competition had produced a winner. Not the one he expected, but a clear winner. Most significantly, he would see his process become the Toyota standard.

In speaking with Kevin Hunter, who currently heads CALTY, he confirms the value of the internal competition, which is indeed a formal part of every new product design:

"The process is extremely valuable, for a number of reasons. Toyota is now a global company. You have to look at ideas that reflect the markets and cultures of the world, and blend the best. Even if you're designing a car for a specific market. The various competing designs have that perspective embedded in them. That's far more valuable than, say, looking at a market and doing focus groups to identify priorities. It also allows Toyota to fully utilize its creative resources in the most optimal way. Finally, it sets up a competitive edge. There's much more of an intense focus and awareness when you know that nothing is being handed to you, that you have to win the business. You have to do your most excellent work. You have no choice: You have to deliver a perfect proposal."

FRAMING: A LOST ART

We frame art to draw attention to the picture. A great frame enhances appreciation. A picture isn't complete without it. But most of us probably don't pay much attention to the frame. Unless, of course, it isn't there. In which case we probably find it a bit tougher to give the piece its proper consideration.

Framing in problem solving is every bit as important. The ability to properly frame an issue or problem goes far in avoiding the typical pitfalls that limit our ability to reach the elegant solution. But it's no easy challenge. Framing is as much an art as art itself. There are plenty of reasons why we're not as good at it as we could be. We're impatient, with attention spans sometimes far too limited to put the required energy toward framing. We're obsessed with solutions, but not with the process of generating the optimal one. We're fond of common sense, which doesn't always square with proper framing. And we have a flair for the obvious, mostly because it provides a suitable mental shortcut.

Example: Turn this incorrect Roman-numeral equation made up of ten sticks into a correct one by moving as few sticks as possible:

$$XI + I = X$$

My guess is you jumped into moving things around right away. Maybe you moved one and came up with X + I = XI. Congratulations. You *satisficed*. The elegant solution? Zero. You don't need to move a single stick. Turn the book upside down.

The point: elegant solutions are discovered by elegant framing.

To become a great problem framer, *focus on asking the right question, not seeking the right answer*. Fight the urge to be prescriptive right away. First think about the diagnosis. You gain no insight by jumping to solutions. Hold the tension. Master it.

Tools can definitely help. Dynamic Tension is a framing tool. You've seen just how powerful it can be in mastering the creative tension needed to innovate.

MENTAL BLOCKS

Studies of brainstorming sessions reveal that idea generation generally stalls after about twenty minutes. At that point most groups stop and turn their attention to evaluating their ideas. However, the research shows that teams with the best ideas don't stop there. They embrace the psychological barrier and manage the stall zone, opening up new channels of widely divergent and enormously creative thinking.

> *Harmony consists of opposing tensions, like that of the bow and the lyre.*
> **Heraclitus**

Thinking is hard work, and in general we'd rather not do too much of it. That's why we satisfice. The result is that we inhibit problem solving not so much from the analytical viewpoint, but from the consideration of a wide variety of options to analyze. When it comes to innovation and elegant problem solving, the question *"What is the best option?"* should never be entertained until the question *"What is possible?"* has been answered.

But we tend to skip over that, because of one reason: *mental blocks.* We all suffer from the mental blocks. Some we create ourselves. Others come from lack of focus. Or focusing on the wrong aspect of the problem. Or poor framing of the issues. Or from lack of proper direction and purpose. Or lack of complete information. Or orders that misdirect our efforts away from the real problem. Or trying to blast through the block instead of walking around it.

Everyone has at some time tackled a complex, wicked problem, penetrated the root cause, and emerged victorious, having solved it definitively with surprising simplicity. So we know we can do it. We just don't manage that creative capability well.

The mental block wall shields the elegant solution, if we let it. Avoiding mental blocks requires a certain mindfulness. It's the perspective used at Toyota. Toyota vice president Mike Morrison puts it this way:

What appears to be the problem, isn't.

What appears to be the solution, isn't.

What appears to be impossible, isn't.

ToolKit: Blockbusting

You're at an impasse. You need something to help you master the creative tension. Try this technique.

Nonlinear Thinking

Inspiration often doesn't come as easily as we'd like it to. Our ideas all seem to head down the same old road we've taken before. This technique may help you go off-road a bit. Give yourself 20 minutes for the whole exercise.

Imagine your team owns a kitchen appliance company, and the problem is marketing the new refrigerator.

Go to the dictionary, open it to any page, and pick the first noun on the page.

Example: Fish.

Now list as many words as you can think of that somehow relate to "fish." Spend 5 minutes.

Example: swim, ocean, fin, frozen, catch, boat, scale, sushi

Pick a few of those associations and relate them back to your problem. Use them to spark ideas and new ways of thinking about refrigerators. This will help you get off the normal path of ideas associated with appliances.

Example: "Frozen" might spur the idea of selling refrigerators to Eskimos to prevent fish from freezing in the Arctic.

Now use the technique with the real problem you're trying to solve!

HANSEI

How do you generate creative tension?

What was your last successful complex challenge addressed?

What key mechanisms were employed to master it?

How do you leverage group intelligence?

What kinds of tools do you use to frame problems and structure thinking?

CHAPTER 11

Run the Numbers

The purpose of computing is insight, not numbers.
R. J. Hamming

Think for Yourself—Temper Instinct with Insight, Focus on Facts, and Do the Math

Problem: *Proposed solutions lack basis in fact.* Innovation is more art than science, or so the thinking goes. And with it goes rationality and reliance on facts to drive key decisions. That makes innovation more risky, because the effort is relegated to a "gut instinct." And that's a problem, because in the absence of solid fact, conventional wisdom usually rules the day. That means the problem does not get the scrutiny, objectivity, and critical analysis it deserves. Given the current rate of change, the tried and true may in reality no longer be true. Without running the numbers, issues don't get the proper analysis. So there will be no elegant solution.

Cause: *Aversion to numbers.* Many people resist using data in solving problems, making decisions, and building plans. Some of it can be traced to how statistics are taught in school. Numbers are presented in such a way that we're either bored to death or scared to death. Either way, we swear off numbers, failing to realize the powerful insights they can provide. That lets assumption, intuition, and personal belief run the show.

Solution: *Counter intuition with insight.* Innovation by definition disrupts the status quo. Digging into relevant data helps fight the dangers of bias, convention, and instinct. There's nothing better to help make the break with comfortable patterns than solid evidence.

Great innovations are based on much more than a feeling.

DOWNFALL OF INSTINCT

Imagine you're a contestant on the old *Let's Make a Deal* game show. Host Monty Hall offers you the chance to win a beautiful new Lexus. It's behind one of three closed doors. Behind each of the other two is a goat.

History Lesson

In September 1991 a reader of Marilyn vos Savant's column in the Sunday magazine *Parade* posed this very question. Marilyn answered correctly that the contestant should switch doors. Her answer provoked nearly 10,000 responses from readers, most of them disagreeing with her. Several were from mathematicians and scientists whose responses lamented the nation's lack of math skills, and who later had to retract their statements.

You choose a door, and Monty, who knows where the Lexus is, opens one of the remaining two doors to reveal a goat. He offers you a choice: Stay where you are, or switch to the other closed door. *What do you do?*

Instinct says we have a 50-50 shot, so why switch, right? Wrong. Always switch. Our odds double. Hard to believe, until we run the numbers!

There are only two scenarios, *stay* and *switch*. Each has three possibilities as shown below. But not really, because Monty knows where the car is. Here's how it works. Let's say you pick door #1. Monty opens any door without a Lexus behind it.

If you run through each three-door possibility in the "Stay" scenario, then do the same with "Switch," the spread looks like this:

STAY			
Door 1	Door 2	Door 3	Result
Lexus	Goat	Goat	**WIN**
Goat	Lexus	Goat	LOSE
Goat	Goat	Lexus	LOSE

SWITCH			
Door 1	Door 2	Door 3	Result
Lexus	Goat	Goat	LOSE
Goat	Lexus	Goat	**WIN**
Goat	Goat	Lexus	**WIN**

You have twice the odds of winning if you switch!

Remember, Monty will never reveal the car. He'll always show you a goat. So while intuition says *two doors, 50-50 shot, stay put*—running the numbers shows the downfall of instinct.

So don't just "blink," think! And always do the math.

The Dangers

What we generally refer to as instinct or intuition isn't a mysterious force or extrasensory perception. And it doesn't come from our gut, it comes from the soft-wired patterns in our brains. Our brains are powerful pattern makers, perpetually recognizing and constructing unconscious patterns, unbeknownst to us.

Intuition is a tapestry of unconscious patterns in action. Each of us holds a unique set of patterns that form our special point of view, our personal mindset built on our collective experiences in life.

Here's how it works. Every new experience is automatically stored as data in our brain, to be grouped with other like data as it comes in. The groupings become patterns. Mental models. Paradigms. Experience is the input; patterns in the form of unconscious beliefs that govern our thoughts and behaviors are the output.

The good news is that intuition mostly works in a good way by helping us quickly arrive at the correct answer and take the best course of action. It's especially useful for handling routine problems that don't require deeper thought. Intuition is a huge part of our intelligence, and we'd be rather useless without it. It helps us rapidly sift and sort information into useful knowledge, according to whether it confirms or contradicts the strong patterns already embedded in our minds.

But therein lies the downside for innovative problem solving. A few everyday examples prove the point.

Remote Rote

When we want to watch television, we aim the remote at the box without even thinking about it. We instinctively know from the countless times of doing so that pressing the power button will convert the "TV off" pattern to the "TV on" pattern. When the television doesn't come on, we keep hitting the power button repeatedly until we're certain it won't work, defending our mindset. Then a new pattern kicks in: Play with the batteries. We don't replace them, we roll them around, then revert to the first action of aiming the remote at the TV. Only when doing so doesn't work will we replace the batteries, again reverting to the first mindset. If that doesn't work, we run down the list of what's worked in the past, still not really thinking or analyzing the situation. Only when we've exhausted every known fix will we attempt a more objective problem-solving effort and start asking ourselves: Why doesn't the remote work?

Alien Action

You're playing a video game that gives you a choice: Fight the alien super-warrior or three human soldiers in a row. The game informs you that your probability of defeating the alien superwarrior is 1 in 7. The probability of defeating a human soldier is 1 in 2. What do you do? Most people would fight the human soldiers. It seems to make intuitive sense. The odds seem to be in your favor. But they're not. Your probability of winning three battles in a row would be 1/2 X 1/2 X 1/2, or 1/8. You have a better shot at beating the alien superwarrior. It's a simple problem of probability.

In these quick examples, what leads us astray, gets in the way, and prevents us from solving the problem on the first pass is our reflexive thinking. We know the answer *intuitively*. Generally speaking, as soon as we recognize a piece of information as being a part of a preexisting pattern, our mental models work to shortcut our thinking—unconsciously jumping us ahead to a plausible conclusion. They then continue to work as a filter, screening in any information that supports our conclusion, screening out any information that conflicts with it or leads to another possibility. By nature, the mind stays closed as long as possible!

The bottom line is that we tend to see only what we believe. That's not good. When we limit our thinking to just what we believe, innovative thinking becomes a moonshot. Convention is convention because everyone *believes* it. Innovation runs counter to convention, counter to intuition. And that's the danger.

While it works fine for routine or benign problems, *instinct must be tempered with insight to solve tough problems.*

Perspective

Patterns appear in everything from atoms to art. It is mathematics that enables us to recognize them. Mathematics is really the science of patterns, not numbers.

Everyone sees patterns every day. We mostly just take them for granted. We ignore their power to explain, diagnose, and solve.

Mathematicians don't. They see patterns within patterns.

So do the best innovators.

SAFETY IN NUMBERS

One way to counterbalance intuition and battle convention is to fight fire with fire. Convention and intuition are close cousins, conglomerates of patterns. So you need patterns to handle it all.

Luckily, we're natural pattern lovers, because we prefer order over chaos, and patterns indicate an underlying system of order. Patterns offer a logical explanation for what we observe. Patterns are inescapable, so it's in our interest to get good at using them to solve problems.

We can do that by running the numbers. That's how we discover patterns. And the real power of patterns is *predictability*. Risk is inherent in business innovation at any level, so it makes sense to think about predictability as a way of handling risk.

Stories of innovative approaches founded in numbers reveal just how critical it is to use some sort of mathematical method.

Google

Google, perhaps the most prevalent example of an elegant solution, began as a math problem. The name itself springs from a number—a googol is a 1 followed by 100 zeros. Google sprang from an attempt to understand and explain the Web in mathematical terms by Sergey Brin and Larry Page in their paper *The Anatomy of a Large-Scale Hypertextual Web Search Engine,* which described PageRank, the basis of their search engine.

> We look at what the Web thinks. What do other pages say? It's a pretty good measure that it's the right page, because the whole world thinks it's the right page.
>
> **Larry Page**

Brin and Page had noticed a market inefficiency: Search engines like high-flying dot-com Yahoo! were all the rage, but they were too simplistic and ineffective in handling complex searches. Most were based on human maintenance, too subjective, slow to improve, useless for more esoteric searches, and expensive to build and update. Using a century-old mathematical tool called a Markov chain, named for mathematician Andrei Markov, they set out to understand how pages on the Web linked to each other. The goal was to find a simple solution to the question: *How can I find and sort the Web sites most relevant to my search?*

No one had ever used Markov chains to examine the Web. Their work culminated in a mathematical ranking of connections based on the number of times a page is cited or linked to. That ran counter to prevailing search engines that simplistically counted key word repetition on a page. It was a dynamic ranking based on how the Web was connected. The exact formula is secret, of course, but their solution was an equation that took into account the number of pages linking to a specific site page, the number of pages leading out of that page, and the chance that a user may not follow links sequentially, but start their search all over. The rest is history. Google is a marketplace phenomenon.

Oakland A's

Oakland A's general manager Billy Beane discovered how to trump conventional wisdom and consistently outperform the competition by taking a statistical approach to America's pastime and objectively analyzing the factors that actually produce runs. Runs, after all, win games. The A's had the lowest budget in baseball, so the central question driving Beane's discovery was intriguing and relevant in today's fierce business environment: *How can I do more with less?*

The answer required an elegant solution. The approach was mathematical. First, examine the vital statistics that determine whether you win or not; in this case, runs. Focus on what leads to runs; in this case, getting on base. Second, search for the factors that produce results but get little attention; in this case, walks. Third, shed the conventional strategies that statistically just don't work; in this case, stolen bases.

> *I have no data yet. It is a capital mistake to theorize before one has data. Insensibly one begins to twist facts to suit theories instead of theories to suit facts.*
> **Sherlock Holmes**

The data showed that traditional scouting targets were overvalued and suboptimizing. Young hot pitchers, speedy base runners, and big hitters didn't win games. It wasn't so much about athleticism as it was about batters who could manage the strike zone and get on base a high percentage of the time. By simply focusing on the facts, he rewrote the rules and changed the game.

Lance Armstrong

Following his bout with testicular cancer, Lance Armstrong found that his physiology had changed. He was lighter, with a diminished musculature. The way his body most efficiently produced power had changed. He needed a new way to ride the bike in order to compete at the elite level. He examined the power equation of Power = Force x Velocity, where force was the force applied to his pedals and velocity was leg speed, or pedal cadence. He did the math, looking at the variables. *If it takes 200 watts to move a bike at 20 mph, what were the possibilities? What were the differences of pedaling 70 rpm, versus 100 rpm?* Lower cadence required higher force applied to each pedal stroke, which meant more work for his leg muscles, and quicker fatigue. Lower force to the pedals required higher cadence, which meant more work for his heart and aerobic system.

Given his stronger aerobic engine, he switched to spinning lower gears at a much higher cadence. It ran counter to the widely accepted practice of driving big gears while seated. But it worked. No one could touch him in grueling mountain climbs of the Alps and Pyrenees.

Wall Street

Banker and statistician David Li helped change the investment community involved in the credit derivatives market by devising a mathematical model to predict the likelihood that a certain group of corporations would default on their bond debt in quick succession. The enormous multitrillion-dollar credit derivatives market that now rides on assorted versions of Li's original computer model was barely a blip on the radar screen in 1995.

In 1997, Li began pondering a single question: *Why do many elderly people die so soon after their beloved spouses do?* That was just about the time investment banks began pooling corporate bonds and selling slices of the pool, like mortgages. You could buy a risky slice, or a safe slice. Higher risk meant potentially higher return, and vice versa. That meant the banks had to estimate the probability of all companies in a given slice taking a dive at the same time, in order to figure the likelihood of default.

Nobody knew how to do that, until David Li discovered a solution by investigating what actuaries call the broken-heart factor: the death correlation between the passing of one spouse and the other. Li saw the bond pool default correlation as the exact same problem. He began using copulas, mathematical formulas predicting the likelihood of somewhat dependent events occurring together.

Li published a paper in a financial journal, and it caught the eye of Wall Street. The investment firm Morgan Stanley has hailed the beauty of the model, saying, "It's the simplicity."

PayPal

PayPal, the highly successful email payment program used widely by the millions of small businesses housed on eBay, began as a data pattern.

Young technologist Max Levchin loved the mathematical challenge of breaking codes. He turned his passion to profit by building hacker-proof software encryption. In the late 1990s, skepticism over online payments was still high. "Snail mailing" checks was still the predominant means of buying goods online. That was hugely inefficient for all the budding online marketers signing up for eBay. The auction site was real-time, so the payment method had to match.

Levchin designed PayPal as a way of sending an email payment from buyer to seller following a software authorization to charge the buyer's bank account or credit card. That meant monitoring the program for fraud. No one would use PayPal if it wasn't crime-proof. He needed an antifraud program that would monitor transactions and warn of suspicious accounts.

To observe online thieves, track patterns, and develop a solution that worked, Levchin first had to let Web fraudsters rob him of money. It was risky, but it worked. He began noticing counter-intuitive fraud patterns: correlations between geographic locations, between time zones, among nighttime transactions, between passwords.

The resulting program, Igor, was so successful in preventing fraud based on data patterns that the U.S. government uses it to help solve online

Freaky Figures

Economist Steven Levitt's innovative look at numbers and patterns in his book *Freakonomics* laid to rest the traditional view of mathematics as boring. Using forensic statistics, Levitt focused on the data patterns within patterns that solve curious mysteries and prove conventional thinking wrong, taking on public-school teachers, Sumo wrestlers, real estate agents, parents, and drug dealers.

fraud cases elsewhere. Says Levchin: *"Humans are extremely good at pattern recognition. Computers are only as good as programmed, which is a shame."*

Which is something Jeff Hawkins, creator of the Palm Pilot and Handspring Treo, aims to tackle through his new company, Numenta. Numenta's stated goal is to get computers to recognize patterns and make predictions based on those patterns. Hawkins says that's how the brain works. Scientists agree.

> We have a few intuitive but incorrect assumptions that mislead us. The biggest mistake is the belief that intelligence is defined by intelligent behavior.
> **Jeff Hawkins**

That's the essence of intelligence.

TOOLKIT: THE SLACK POINT

What all these cases have in common is what we might appropriately term the *slack point.* The slack point is an undetected and counterintuitive inefficiency found through analysis of data. It indicates slack in the system. You do not need to be a statistician or mathematician to understand and discover your own slack point.

Here's how Toyota did it at the retail level.

In the late 1990s a southern Toyota dealer had a problem. He was outgrowing his facility. The store was selling 1600 new vehicles a year, and generating $2 million from parts and accessories and $1.5 million in service. The symptoms of the problem were becoming serious; expansion was a looming threat, as was the nearly $500,000 in parts inventory, 10% of which was obsolete. He needed space. And money.

Seeking help for the expansion effort, the general manager called the Customer Services Department's Dealer Development group of the North American Parts Logistics Division at Toyota Motor Sales headquarters.

Logistics professionals arrived on the scene and immediately noticed a possible slack point in the service and parts operation. Service technicians spent a good bit of time at the parts counter waiting for parts. They decided to collect data. Over the course of a week, they determined that waiting time at the parts window wasted nearly 19 hours per day. Each trip took on average five minutes. With five teams of five technicians each making an average of nine visits per day lasting five minutes per visit, the slack point was confirmed. Part of the slack point was due to the visit itself, the other was due to an inefficient parts system. The inventory was stacked according to convention, based on size and space. That led to wasted search time.

The slack point was attacked directly. The team conducted a study over three months to identify the fastest-moving parts. Data showed that slow-moving parts were the prime cause of the problem.

Solution? 1. Resituate the fastest-moving parts to enable quicker access by putting those parts most often requested nearest the counter to reduce the steps to retrieve them. 2. Implement a just-in-time, sell-one/buy-one method of resupplying parts—source by movement.

Turnaround was immediate. Saving time behind the counter saved time for the service technician. That in turn shortened the time needed to service each vehicle, thereby increasing customer satisfaction and output, meaning more revenue to grow the dealership.

The new supply system allowed the parts and accessories department to reduce parts inventory by 35% and order parts on demand. That in turn freed up 30% of the storage space for other uses.

Dramatic improvement in time, efficiency, and productivity led to impressive bottom-line gains within 18 months: Obsolete parts inventory was reduced from $50,000 to $8000. Parts sales grew 50%. Service department appointment scheduling went from 7 days to 3. An additional service team was added. Monthly service sales grew 25%, with 45% increase in gross profit contribution.

Elimination of the slack point resulted in new service bays and expanded hours. All because of slow-moving parts.

> **Most of the concepts and patterns that are difficult for the average person to grasp and use are nonintuitive.**
> **Morton Hunt**

No one could have told the general manager that he would be able to realize such gains simply by shifting parts around behind the counter and eliminating time spent by service technicians waiting at the parts counter.

Because intuition and instinct would have told him otherwise.

THE MAGIC NUMBER

Numbers can be magic. But any old numbers won't do. It has to be the right set of numbers for your business. The right number can turn everything around. It can *be* the elegant solution.

In his book *The One Thing You Need to Know,* Marcus Buckingham counsels us to find a "core score." He tells the story of the newly appointed chief inspector of the British prison system who achieved a dramatic turnaround by simply changing the measure of success from number of escapees to number of repeat offenders. Counterintuitive and world-changing!

There's plenty of useless data collected in surveys. We end up ignoring it, and rightfully so. The problem is that we too often ignore the useful data in favor of our experience and emotion.

And that's when convention, instinct, and intuition creep into the equation masquerading as common sense. That's when we begin to collect data meant only to confirm our belief system. That's when belief blocks objectivity. That's when it gets dangerous.

Consultant Ian Mitroff attributes General Motors's dramatic loss of market share in the 1980s at the hands of import car companies to a decades-old, multilevel mindset: *Styling and status is more important than quality; foreign cars are no threat; and workers don't make a difference.* All of their data confirmed those assumptions...because the surveys were designed to! The mindset was built in. Conventional thinking reigned supreme. GM became aware of its faulty thinking only when it was far too late.

Toyota Production System engineer Taiichi Ohno maintained that common sense is the enemy, and advocated four things in fighting intuition:

1. *Always temper immediate action.*

2. *Resist drawing conclusions on emotion.*

3. *Question hearsay.*

4. *Draw from experience, but don't rely on it solely.*

Unless we learn to discipline ourselves to run the numbers, becoming truly objective will always remain elusive. So whatever you do, do your math.

Hansei

What is the slack point in your business?

What patterns might be investigated to challenge convention?

What key measures define success in your business?

What critical success factors are undervalued?

How well do the data support your decision?

CHAPTER 12

Make Kaizen Mandatory

What drives men of genius is their obsession with the idea that what has
already been done is still not enough.

Eugène Delacroix

Pursuing Perfection Requires Great Discipline—
Create a Standard, Follow It, and Find a Better Way

Problem: *Innovation is hit or miss.* It's ad hoc. It's not widespread. It's
a long shot. For many, it's a pipe dream.

Cause: *Creativity is misdirected and mismanaged.* Combined research
from the Employee Involvement Association and Japan Human Relations
Association reveals that the average number of ideas submitted per
employee annually is 100 times greater in Japanese companies than in U.S.
companies. Why? For one thing, we reward the wrong thing in the wrong
way. The average reward in Japanese companies is 100 times less than the
average U.S. reward of nearly $500. We have it backward! The bottom line
is that the Western business practice of rewarding only accepted ideas has
all but killed the creative drive of corporate America.

Solution: *Embed the kaizen ethic.* Kaizen (ky-zen), the Japanese word
for continuous improvement, is all about idea submission, not
acceptance. The *de facto* incubator for consistent business innovation, it's
the practice that fosters a strong ethos of lablike curiosity in companies
like Toyota. And it's a proven, grassroots way to harvest human creativity.

Kaizen has three steps: First, create a standard. Second, follow it.
Third, find a better way. Repeat endlessly. Trying to improve and
innovate without a standard as reference is like a journey with no starting
point. It's like hitting golf balls in the fog.

KAIZEN DEMYSTIFIED

Misconceptions abound with respect to the concept of kaizen. It's a *Japanese* thing. It's a *Toyota* thing. It's a *quality* thing. It's an *efficiency* thing. It's a *manufacturing* thing.

None of which are true.

With all due respect to Japan and Toyota, the simple truth is that kaizen is just a word the Japanese came up with a half century ago for something the U.S. military taught Japan during the U.S. Occupation in the aftermath of World War II. But it's an elegant word. Kaizen is one of those magical concepts that is at once a philosophy, a principle, a practice, and a tool. And it's in the *Oxford English Dictionary,* so it can't be all that Japanese.

> *Kaizen activities are the incubator of innovation. This is because Kaizen activities create an atmosphere of accepting change.*
> **Akira Takahashi**

Let's look closer, because kaizen has everything to do with ingenuity, perfection, and fit.

Kaizen: American-Made

The best way to illuminate kaizen is through a quick history lesson. Knowing where it came from, and that it's an American-made approach to innovation, helps remove the mystique that can block adoption.

Three factors came together to help embed the kaizen ethic in Japanese business DNA during the decade or so following the war: The United States Air Force, General Douglas MacArthur, and quality statistician Dr. W. Edwards Deming. Here's the short course.

When France fell to Hitler's Third Reich in 1940 and U.S. involvement in the European theater looked imminent, U.S. manufacturers needed ways to ramp up production. The U.S. government under Roosevelt formed an emergency service called Training Within Industries Service (TWI) to help quickly boost production and productivity. Three programs were developed: Job Instruction Training, Job Relations Training, and Job Methods Training. Job Methods Training (JMT) taught how to generate and implement ideas through hundreds of small changes that could be effected immediately. The term used for the method was continuous improvement. The focus was on improving the current work and existing equipment, because there simply wasn't time for large-scale ideas or design of new tools.

Training happened rapidly, using a train-the-trainer approach. A handful of course developers each taught two trainers, who in turn trained twenty instructors. TWI trained over 2 million supervisors in less than five years.

Enter Dr. W. Edwards Deming, a statistician and protegé of 1930s statistician Walter Shewhart. A huge advocate of continuous improvement, Deming was part of a quality control team helping manufacturers during the war. He preached the involvement of everyone in the effort, not just supervisors and managers.

Little stuff, not enough, right? You need the big swags to close the gap fast, right? No. It was a brilliant solution. Quality, cost, and speed were improved 25% across the board. Students of history know that the superior equipment quality and production line speed figured heavily in the Allied defeat of the Axis forces.

TWI vanished after the end of the war. But the approach followed General MacArthur's occupation forces in Japan as the United States began to help rebuild the devastated nation. As an economy, Japan had no business game going at that time. Beyond the battle wreckage, they didn't know how to run a business. No standards. Haphazard management. No training. No employee involvement. MacArthur needed to jump-start the economy, for a number of reasons. Civil unrest was a threat, as were starvation, interruption to supply lines, communist invasion from North Korea. He needed to replicate the wartime success of TWI. The government sent him TWI, Inc., a company founded by one of the original TWI service instructors.

Dr. Deming arrived in Japan in 1950 at the invitation of the Japanese Union of Scientists and Engineers, and immediately began teaching and consulting on the principles of statistical quality control and continuous improvement using The Scientific Method, or Shewhart Cycle, as he termed it: Plan, Do, Study, Act. Not unlike the disappearance of TWI, his strategies were largely ignored in the United States following the end of the war.

Around the same time, the United States Air Force developed a training program to help the Japanese workers employed to run the main logistics and matériel depot. The workforce was poorly disciplined with respect to safety, work habits, and equipment operation. A training program was developed, called, appropriately enough, Management Training Program. It employed a philosophy closely matched to Dr. Deming's: Everyone is responsible for improvement and innovation; there is no end to improvements.

Japan soaked it all up. They had no resources. The industrial base had been vaporized. They knew they had been defeated by superior thinking. So they listened. Yes, listening to employee ideas was uncomfortable. Yes, tapping employee creativity was a foreign concept. But they tried it. It worked, so they kept at it, made it habit. And they spread the word about continuous improvement. Quality, productivity, and innovation in Japan took off.

They dubbed the approach kaizen.

KAIZEN BASIS: STANDARDIZATION

The basis of Kaizen is standardized work. You begin by creating a standard. Then you follow it while actively searching for a better way.

The thought of *standards* makes a lot of people cringe. That's because they confuse standardization with uniformity. They think standards somehow discourage creativity. They perceive standards as a control mechanism to prevent individuals from performing the job in the manner they view as best. They see standards as restrictive and rigid, even oppressive.

Developed and used properly, a standard is none of those things. The skepticism and cynicism stems from the fact that in most organizations, standards *are* all those evil things. Most companies use central committees to develop standards. They use the words *standard* and *edict* interchangeably. They issue what is essentially a performance script and call it a standard. The standard is, in effect, permanent. Big mistake.

A true standard is the exact opposite. The difference at companies like Toyota that believe in the kaizen way is this:

- *Standards are created by the individuals performing the work.*
- *Standards are dynamic, and not everything gets standardized.*

A standard is simply an established best-known method or practice followed until a better way is discovered, tested, and accepted. A standard lets you know where there's a problem. It shows you where to begin the search for solutions. It prevents mistakes from being made twice. It lets you capture and retain knowledge and expertise. And it helps you stay safe.

Let's look at what conventional wisdom holds to be exempt from a standardized approach: *design.*

Standardizing Design

Most designers would balk at the hint of standardizing the design process. For all the reasons just covered. *It's much too creative. Much too artistic. Design standards are too old-school. Too slow for today's go-go world. Too stifling.*

At Toyota, the design process is standardized. But it's *not* a paint-by-numbers approach. It's high-level, phase-driven, and allows individual style to enter into how the process is actually executed. It's like driving a car. There are certain guidelines in effect and certain actions every driver takes to operate a car, but you can drive in a direction that suits you.

> If you believe that standards are writ in stone, you will fail. You have to believe that standards are there to be changed.
>
> **Yoshio Shima,** Director
> Toyoda Machine Works

The major structural component is a simple check sheet. Toyota has reams of them, to be sure. But once the check sheet is solid, the designer or engineer is off and running. The function and value of the check sheet is clear and compelling: Get everyone on the same page. That's important when you're dealing with hundreds of designers and engineers coming together to pore over a prototype. It's absolutely critical to meeting a required degree of quality with any sort of predictability. It's vital to shortening overlapping development cycles, because the standard eliminates a lengthy "clean sheet" approach.

Design standards at Toyota are refreshed at regular and frequent times, in part due to the nature of the business: face-lifts come out every year, with major changes every few years. There's no chance for aging or going stale. The design standards are living, breathing instruments constantly changing, continuously updated and improved *each time* by the designer or engineer in the role. As a result, crucial information flows freely. Such standards enable the knowledge, mastery, and creativity of the designer to be captured and shared.

As Sakichi Toyoda once said: *"Let your future be lit with the knowledge of the past."*

French Kaizen

You read it right. Kaizen, not cuisine.

The northern French firm FAVI is a small 60-year-old copper foundry and manufacturer of automotive gearbox forks. Not only does FAVI profit in markets where its competitors either lose money or slash production costs through Asian outsourcing, it consistently lowers its prices. How?

They practice kaizen. Which makes them an anomaly, especially in a country fond of centralization. The central chain-of-command structure is missing from FAVI. Workers are encouraged to make decisions and take quick action to improve their daily work. Equipment, tooling, workspace, and process redesign rests in the hands of the frontline workers—workers who are known for working off-shift to serve customers and test out new procedures.

FAVI leader Jean-Françoise Zobrist long ago recognized that most corporate hierarchy blocks innovation from below, because the higher-ups are busy managing risk. Not to the company, to their résumé. In fact, FAVI has had no personnel department for two decades, viewing such a structure as an unnecessary constraint on human activity.

The message to FAVI workers is clear: Management doesn't pay them, the customer does. Workers aren't told how to do their jobs; rather, they're reminded of who they're serving and why. Like Toyota factories, the company is basically flat and organized into teams, each with a single designated customer. Control rests with the front lines, where it adds the most value.

FAVI workers are free to experiment, innovate, and solve problems for customers. The only demand is a familiar one for followers of kaizen: faster, better, cheaper, smarter. Always.

Thanks to employees, the cost to produce a copper gearbox fork is nearly half what it was twenty years ago.

The Battle for Standards

A new battle over standards is shaping up, reminiscent of the 1970s'-era Sony Betamax-Matsushita VHS videotape formatting war. We all know who won that one: The superior but more costly and complex Beta format lost out to the inferior but simpler and cheaper VHS format.

Today's war for automotive hybrid technology looks much the same, from a strategic perspective.

In one corner we have Toyota's design, which utilizes electric power as the primary propulsion schema over a wider range of speeds. In the other corner we have General Motors's hybrid design, which utilizes gasoline power as the primary propulsion schema over a wider range of speeds. With respect to fuel efficiency, Toyota's technology is superior but more complex and costly. GM's technology is inferior but simpler and cheaper.

The Toyota system's reliance on electricity yields far greater power and fuel economy, but the electrical componentry is much heavier and more expensive to produce. That poses a problem for larger vehicles like trucks and SUVs. The GM's system is lighter but less powerful and easier on the wallet, and fuel economy isn't nearly as impressive in offering a 25% gain in miles per gallon versus Toyota's over 50% improvement.

Other players like Honda and hybrid component suppliers will figure heavily. GM has commissioned a study of the Beta-VHS war to gain insight. Toyota has licensed its technology to Ford, upped its stake in hybrid supplier Panasonic EV Energy to 60%, and awarded a huge transaxle contract to supply partner Aisin AW, which limits Aisin's capacity to supply others. Rival Ford is particularly miffed at losing the tactical war.

Stay tuned. The skirmish should be quite enlightening and entertaining to watch.

ToolKit: Creating a Standard

You now know the kaizen process: Create a standard, follow it, find a better way. Then repeat forever. You can see how it meets up with IDEA Loops in the D phase. A standard is part of the desired outcome and solution. You can see how IDEA Loops can be a mechanism to drive the kaizen process. The question becomes how to create a standard. Which begs the question of what defines a good one.

Whether it's a pilot's preflight checklist, a surgeon's protocol, or an autoworker's guide to drivetrain assembly, there are two criteria:

A. Clarity

Assume an untrained eye will read it. Make it bulletproof, specific, and complete, to capture the knowledge. Make it concrete and representative of the real world. Describe with precision the what, where, and how. That way, there's no question of what constitutes a problem.

B. Consensus

Everyone who will employ the standard must agree on it. That forces a shared investigation to ensure that the standard represents the best-known method or practice at that specific point in time. The activity in turn facilitates understanding.

Three basic steps are required to deploy a standard:

1. **Establish** a Best Practice—*Make sure it's the best-known method. Get input and feedback from those doing the work. Get agreement on it.*

2. **Document** the Standard—*Make it visual if you can. Use graphics, check sheets, templates. Post it or publish it so everyone will constantly be aware of it.*

3. **Train** to the Method—*Build a launch plan. Inform everyone. Prepare the needed materials and train people and trainers. Monitor the standard for effectiveness and usage.*

What happens if the standard isn't followed? Investigate! Find out why. Is there a better method? Was training adequate? Are there special circumstances? Redesign it if you need to. And keep searching for a better way.

POWER TO THE PEOPLE

Kaizen is democratic. Of the people, by the people, for the people. It recognizes, respects, and taps the power of the human creative spirit. It locates the creative center and channels it, allowing people to get out in front of change. In fact, the whole issue of resistance to change is minimized under a kaizen system, because kaizen involves everyone in the change itself.

> *It's very good for an idea to be commonplace. The important thing is that a new idea should develop out of what is already there so that it soon becomes an old acquaintance.*
> **Penelope Fitzgerald**

That's why we need it more than ever in our organizations. The current rate of change is every bit the burning platform that faced American industry in 1940. Goals are stretching and resources are shrinking. The customer is speeding up and innovation is slowing down. The effectiveness of the improvement efforts during World War II is undeniable. Any conceivable argument against another such widespread approach doesn't hold water. The "things are more complex now" argument is nonsense. Toyota is proof of that. About the only thing capable of stopping them is, well, themselves. By abandoning kaizen, they become every bit as vulnerable to complacency and lethargy as their current competition. Luckily, doing that would be more difficult than embedding kaizen in the first place.

For reasons as unexplainable as why the TWI methods disappeared in the United States after the war, we maintain this aversion to a kaizen ethic even as we proclaim the need to change and manage change. It's a conundrum. But the solution seems glaringly elegant: Harness the power of people.

Unfortunately, a few things stand in the way. One is our propensity to step on the toes of the frontline worker. The other is our cultural preference for paying for ideas. Both block kaizen. Both neutralize the power of people.

Engineers Know Better: Not!

You want things faster, better, cheaper, smarter. So instead of asking for the ideas of those who know the work best, you hire the industrial engineering guns. It happens all the time. The NUMMI case (Chapter 3) should have convinced you of how just plain wrong that is. One of the magic moments in that case was the shift away from the industrial engineer as expert to the employee as expert.

Starbucks, the world's largest and most successful coffee chain, recently wanted to shave a few seconds off the preparation cycle time. So they turned not to their retail team but to their team of operations engineers. Did they realize gains? Sure. Did they realize the kinds of gains they might have with a kaizen approach? The bet is no. The bet is that with kaizen embedded, the problem would have been recognized and solved long before it came to the attention of the retail operations engineering department director.

Reward: The Forbidden Fruit

The statistics cited at the beginning of the chapter point out the diametrically opposed Eastern and Western beliefs regarding the role that monetary reward plays in idea generation. The research is clear: Payment for ideas defeats the purpose. The situation brings to mind a favorite parable:

An old woman lived alone on a street where boys played noisily every afternoon. One day, the din became too much, and she called the boys into her house. She told them she liked to listen to them play, but her hearing was failing and she could no longer hear their games. She asked them to come around each day and play noisily in front of her house. If they did, she would give them each a quarter. The youngsters raced back the following day, and they made a tremendous racket playing happily in front of the house. The old woman paid and asked them to return the next day. Again they played and made noise, and again she paid them for it. But this time she gave each boy only 20 cents, explaining that she was running out of money. On the following day, they got only 15 cents each. Furthermore, the old woman told them she would have to reduce the fee to a nickel on the fourth day. The boys then became angry and said they would not be back. It was not worth the effort, they said, to play for only a nickel a day.

The fable should ring a familiar bell.

The old woman's scheme effectively stole from the boys the very thing they loved most to do, what they were in fact doing for free. The moral of the story is pretty clear. If we're not careful, we can replace a natural motivation with a synthetic one. We can rob creative power from people by attaching a financial reward to ideas.

The story repeats itself all the time. Companies treat employees like rats in a maze after cheese, by paying for approved ideas and accepted suggestions. They then wonder why they get such low participation. They give no thought to the notion that in order to get a good idea, you need a lot of ideas.

Teachers are notorious for the practice. They want students to read more books, so they reward the completion of books. Maybe with a homework exemption. Or extra credit. Or even vouchers to the local Taco Bell. So the quick and easy books get read. The superficial books get read. Even the good readers, the ones who love to read, get swept up in the program. They stop reading the classics, turning to the quick reads to score points. Then the program is discontinued, and everyone stops reading. Even the best readers lose their love of words. And that's a true shame.

Kaizen aims to draw out the natural curiosity and creativity within people and guide it toward adding value for customers. Kaizen does not attempt to light a fire under people.

It lights the fire *within* them.

ONE MORE THING

Kaizen is very, very hard. You're up against a powerful foe: the end of the month. Or quarter, whichever the case may be in your organization. That forces a short-term perspective, which is at odds with a long view. That's why most companies shy away from it.

> I think we have arrived at where we are through engaging in new things with daring.
> **Eiji Toyoda**

Fight it.

If you don't, you stand no chance at all of keeping the flame of innovation alive. Know that kaizen is at heart about people. *People*

Perspective

"When you improve a little each day, eventually big things occur. When you improve conditioning a little each day, eventually you have a big improvement in conditioning. Not tomorrow, not the next day, but eventually, a big gain is made. Don't look for the big, quick improvement. Seek the small improvement one day at a time. That's the only way it happens—and when it happens, it lasts."

—John Wooden

innovate, companies don't. You have to change attitudes to make it work. That takes a deep commitment, and a lot of time, plus a lot of education.

Start with standards. They make life easier. They create real and lasting value—certainly for your customers.

What electronics consumer wouldn't love for someone to come out with a standard AC power adapter for their myriad gadgets and gizmos? Who isn't tired of lugging around all the black boxes? Who isn't tired of struggling with the black boxes that don't play nice with the other black boxes on the power strip you're trying to plug into? Who isn't tired of power strips?

So do it. Make kaizen mandatory.

Establish the best, safest, easiest, most effective way to do something today. Anything, it doesn't matter what. Just start somewhere and put the stake in the ground. Let everyone know where you and they stand. Don't worry if it's not the gold standard. Keep practicing it, studying it and improving it, and one day it will be. Then you'll look back on where you started and amaze yourself with just how innovative you are.

But know this: You're never done.

HANSEI

How are new ideas encouraged in your organization?

Where do your best ideas come from?

How do you sustain idea flow?

How free are employees to improve the work?

To what degree are standards employed?

CHAPTER 13

Keep It Lean

Simplicity is the ultimate sophistication.
Leonardo da Vinci

Complexity Kills—Scale It Back, Make It Simple, and Let It Flow

Problem: *Too many, too much—of everything.* Too many features, choices, and steps. Too much information, too much to think about. Too much time and too many delays. If you want to benefit society, find ways to eradicate complexity and simplify life. Your business will grow. Your customers will thank you. And never leave.

Cause: *Assumption that more is better.* More is often just more. Unless it's more simple, accessible, timely, and efficient, which really means it's less complicated and complex.

When it comes to solutions, size and sprawl matter. Be-all, end-all, feature-rich solutions almost always miss the mark. Because they're over-scoped and too complex. They're usually proof that we lack real insight into our customer's desires. Complexity destroys value, which is what matters most to the customer. The most elegant solutions always seem blazingly simple. So simple they evoke a slap to the forehead: *"That's so obvious. It's just what I needed. Why didn't I think of that?"* But, as Oliver Wendell Holmes said, the key is "simplicity on the other side of complexity." So how do you get there?

Solution: *Start thinking lean.* Build your solution from the customer back and drive out anything connected to complexity. Because there is absolutely nothing elegant in excess.

What Lean Means

Lean gets to the heart of elegance through simplicity. Regardless of whether the perspective is professional or personal, lean is about one thing: *doing more of what matters by eliminating what doesn't.*

Lean is an application of Toyota's way of starting with the ideal and little by little removing everything blocking the path to achieving it. It captures what Antoine de Saint-Exupéry once said: *"Perfection is achieved not when there is nothing more to add, but when there is nothing left to take away."*

It's a different way of thinking. A different way of approaching work and life. That's why so many companies can't quite get lean, no matter what they do.

They're looking at the problem the wrong way.

Roots of Lean

On the professional business front, we have James P. Womack and Daniel T. Jones to thank for popularizing the term *Lean Thinking* in their 1996 book of the same name. It was their expression for what they observed by studying Toyota's manufacturing processes: an absence of waste.

Meant to convey the essence of the Toyota Production System, the lean concept has moved beyond the factory floor to become an organizing principle and practice that seeks to fully engage the entire workforce in creating and delivering the highest possible customer value through relentless innovation. Processes are streamlined and problems are solved, with the goal of flowing benefit to the customer in the most optimal way possible to free them from the tyranny of complexity.

Perspective

Michelangelo was once asked how he sculpted his marble masterpiece, the statue of David, considered to be the image of the perfect man, to which he replied: *"I saw David through the stone, and I simply chipped away everything that was not David."*

Legendary IBM boss Tom J. Watson Jr. was once asked how to achieve excellence, to which he replied: *"Quit doing less-than-excellent work."*

Best-selling business author Jim Collins once said that *"A great piece of art is composed not just of what is in the final piece, but equally important, what is not. It is the discipline to discard what does not fit—to cut out what might have already cost days or even years of effort—that distinguishes the truly exceptional artist and marks the ideal piece of work, be it a symphony, a novel, a painting, a company or, most important of all, a life."*

On the personal side of the coin, lean shows up in the simplicity movement, which encourages shedding the excess of extravagance. Grassroots "Voluntary Simplicity" took hold in the Pacific Northwest during the early 1990s, but can be traced to 18th-century "Yankee frugality" and Henry David Thoreau's urge to "Simplify, simplify, simplify!"

> *The ability to simplify means to eliminate the unnecessary so that the necessary may speak.*
> **Hans Hoffman**

The movement claims that over 15% of the adult population in the United States practices some form of voluntary simplicity.

It's Not Easy, Being Lean

Lean is often much easier to describe than define. And it's easier to describe what it isn't than what it is. Lean isn't about cost cutting. Or slashing prices. Or workforce reduction. Or beating up suppliers to get the lowest price. Or manufacturing processes only. Or anything related to being spartan, skinny, or stingy.

Lean is observable, but intangible. It's more a state of mind than anything. It's a certain consciousness about doing more with, and for, less. It's more about optimizing than maximizing.

There's only one way to think lean: counterintuitively. We are hardwired to hunt, gather, and hoard. To think *more*. So lean runs counter to human nature. Getting lean requires fighting the basic instinct to add, accumulate, and store.

Lean requires a precise understanding of value: the who, what, when, where, how, and why of the customer's need.

It then means getting that value to them without complexity creeping in.

Lean Ain't Mean

Lean requires innovative thinking. Cost cutting doesn't. Facing financial difficulty in 2005, Northwest Airlines announced its big "lean" plan to compete with the Southwests and JetBlues of the world. The story made headlines in the *Wall Street Journal*.

Phase 1: discontinue free meals.

Phase 2: discontinue free pretzels and magazines.

Phase 3: sell trail mix for one dollar.

Savings? $2 million. First quarter loss? $450 million.

Pulling pretzels isn't lean. It's mean.

The Power of Lean: "Just What I Needed"

It's just what I needed. Getting it was effortless.

That's some of the highest praise customers can sing. It just doesn't get much better than that. That's when you know you've delivered what they value to them at the right time, to the right place, in the right form, in the right way, with the right quality and price. That's when you know that push has become pull, that your operation is in peak flow, and that you've solved their problem in a most elegant way.

And it doesn't matter how you define a customer. Be it a consumer, the next process, another division—everyone is a customer today. There's little choice but to understand value through their eyes and deliver it in a manner that works for them.

True lean is rare. Very rare. You know you're lean when: *Customers pull compelling value from you effortlessly.* To get there, you have to wage an all-out war on complexity. That assumes you've got a handle on your value proposition.

Complexity comes in three basic flavors, all of which impede the frictionless flow of value to customers in an on-demand way, and all of which are the express targets of a lean approach:

1. *Inconsistency.* Anything uneven, imbalanced or irregular.

2. *Overload.* Any excessive or unreasonable burden.

3. *Waste.* Anything that unnecessarily depletes the resources of time, effort, space, and money. This is the biggest obstacle to elegant solutions. It's a poison pill on both the supply and demand side of the equation.

The practices we've covered thus far will help you wage war on the elements of complexity. For, you see, we've come full circle in our discussion of the principles and practices used to pursue the elegant solution through everyday innovation.

Two final cases illustrate the power of thinking lean: one from Toyota, one not. Each describes an elegant solution.

Lean Homebuilding: The Quadrant Story

Few homebuilders can claim that they start and finish seven homes a day, every day. Or build a home in 54 days at $32 per square foot while knowing with precision where each house is on any given day in the construction process. Or claim a nearly 40% referral rate while realizing over 18% return on investment. Or have people camping out on the doorstep of the sales office days before a new development is released.

Weyerheuser subsidiary Quadrant Homes of Seattle, Washington can. But they didn't always. In the late 1990s they nearly went out of business as a residential spec home builder.

Luckily, they learned to think lean. They're now Seattle's number one home builder.

Quadrant Homes had been at breakeven or worse since the early 1990s. Although ads proclaimed them "The Mark of Distinction," they were indistinguishable from any other residential builder. The process was familiar and conventional: Step one: Buy a tract, assuming high demand and hoping for appreciation. Step two: Design the home from the builder's viewpoint to incorporate housing trends, meet buyer profiles, and match the competition. Step three: Construct the home in 90 to 120 days, which was considered normal. Home options were upgraded at the builder's whim, preventing buyers entering the process late being able to customize. Step four: Sell the home, often making price concessions to incentivize buyers, in turn creating tension between the sales team and production. Step five: Conduct a single, final walkthrough focused on fixing defects and problems to be covered under warranty. Step six: Close the home.

That's standard procedure for most homebuilders today. And while it works passably well in generally high demand areas, Quadrant was up against a new home market that had flatlined. Few of their developments had proved profitable. High inventory costs in the form of buildings in process and infrequent payouts associated with their "big box" planned community strategy made Quadrant essentially a nonperforming Weyerheuser asset. Customer satisfaction was at an all-time low.

Operationally, chaos reigned supreme. Superintendents spent their time wrangling subcontractors and juggling schedules. Activity was irregular, with sites going dormant for days while on other days becoming a buzz of activity as subcontractors bumped into each other. At still other times, workers were found sitting around simply waiting for direction. The entire subcontractor/trade vendor schema ran uncontrolled. High warranty claims and accidents revealed a lack of focus on quality and safety.

The sales process neglected the customer. Depending upon where the buyer entered the scene, little was offered in the way of customization. Those amenities and options that did exist were marked up from 40 to 70%. Homes completed without a buyer were inevitably well above base price advertising due to the installation of top-end options. For the late-entering homebuyer, which was the de facto standard, the home was almost always priced beyond reach.

Weyerheuser was about to pull the plug. Then Quadrant turned everything around.

They studied the market. They found a gaping, unarticulated, unanswered need. A problem to solve. A significant percentage of first-time home buyers wanted more functional space at a lower price. They didn't think they could afford a new home with fancy but useless features, so they bought existing homes, which offered more space for the money. They wanted a mature landscape and an established community. They wanted to avoid the difficult new-home buying process.

In a move reminiscent of Southwest Airlines' strategy of competing not with other airlines but with buses and trains, Quadrant decided to compete with existing homes, not new. That meant a lower price point. That meant a different kind of home. It meant a different value proposition targeted to the exact needs of their new customer group. "More House, Less Money" became the calling card.

But the crowning stroke? The elegant solution? Move the fourth step—selling the home—to the second step in the process. Sell the home, then, and only then, build it.

It was brilliant. By moving a single step, the entire system changed.

Site selection became easier and more abundant, because any fast moving area, new or used, would work. Price points matched the existing home market.   Design shifted from the builder's bias to the customer's: Architecture focused on space and functionality, not design artistry. Each development offered three footprints, each with four floor plans to choose from. The standardized customization offered the flexibility customers wanted while reducing complexity.

Push became pull through the creation of a backlog of pre-sold homes. Like with the Toyota Production System, "sell one, make one" was achievable. A pull system enabled a standardized construction process, and a variable 90 to 120 days was compressed to a standard 54 days that was controlled through selecting a single long-term partner for each trade. The long-term commitment enabled a lower cost structure.

Scheduling moved from the field to the central office, and a simple "stringline" chart showed the progress of each home in process. Like the assembly line in a Toyota factory, delays on one home stopped production on the others to ensure workload leveling and continuous flow. The role of superintendent shifted to site safety, quality of workmanship, and most important, close interaction with home buyers and the sales team. The final walkthrough inspection and "punchlist" was eliminated by three customer site walks at key milestones and weekly customer calls to update progress.

The buyer was involved up front not only in the selection of floor plans, but in upgrading their options through a dedicated New Home Showroom, a stand-alone retail space offering a wide range of choices and a half-dozen scheduled customer visits to ensure satisfaction with every aspect of the interior. All sales efforts were coordinated between onsite sales counselors, New Home Showroom, and superintendents.

The turnaround was difficult. But Quadrant people began understanding that they were in business not to build homes, but to help people realize the American dream.

In 1998, Quadrant began the new system, starting and finishing one home per day. They're now at seven, and moving to ten. That's 2000 homes a year.

All by thinking lean.

Lessons in Lean from Lance

Lance Armstrong struggled to win his fifth Tour de France in 2003. He had run out of hours in the day to train, and too much energy had been spent during the spring shedding the previous winter's weight gain.

Elite sports training demands progression in workload over time. But increasing the load requires increased recovery time in order to avoid overtraining. There comes a point where longer rides and tougher workouts simply don't work. The returns diminish. In fact, performance can recede.

In preparation for Lance's 2004 attempt at an unprecedented sixth Tour victory, coach Chris Carmichael took a lean approach. Training became more about what Lance *wasn't* doing than what he was.

Carmichael realized that old-school training methods lacked specificity, which resulted in inefficient training. Riders would stay in the saddle for six hours or more, but at intensity levels over or under the optimum level needed to yield desired gains. He realized that with more precise goals for each workout, only four hours might be needed to accomplish what once took six. The extra time on the bike wasn't needed or helpful, and just led to fatigue and longer recovery periods. Power meters and heart rate monitors were used to accurately gauge when specific workout goals had been met.

The entire approach focused removing complexity in the form of overload, inconsistency, and waste. Removing the waste in training and nutrition yielded more time for better recovery, which in turn allowed higher intensity training in a much shorter time frame.

Said Carmichael of Lance's 2004 preparation: *"At the highest levels of sport, it takes a huge effort to see a one percent improvement in performance, and no individual change in training or nutrition is solely responsible. Rather, it is the combination of minute modifications that leads to significant gains."*

Armstrong's simplified preparation also gave him more personal time. Too, eliminating the waste from his program gave him more flexibility to handle his active media schedule without compromising preparation or performance.

The result stands for itself. By doing more with less, Lance Armstrong turned convention on its ear, outprepared and outperformed his competition, and reaped the reward of keeping it lean.

Lean Learning: The University of Toyota

The word "university" conjures up images of ivy-covered walls and massive columns supporting Georgian architecture, of curricula and classes, professors, and students. For most corporate universities, that image isn't far off the mark. Most corporate universities pattern themselves after academic institutions in both structure and intent. For most corporate universities, the goal is delivering education. That makes them glorified central training departments. The connection to the company's business is often a stretch. Senior operating executives find themselves wondering whether the high cost is justified, and whether the university concept is a priority or merely a perk.

But the University of Toyota isn't like other corporate universities. It's a study in lean knowledge work.

The University of Toyota, headquartered in Torrance, California, was officially approved by Toyota Motor Sales, USA, Inc. in 1998. It was one of several corporate initiatives comprising the New Era Strategy, a multi-pronged plan to enhance Toyota's competitive advantage in the new millennium in the areas of product planning, sales, marketing, and distribution in the United States.

True to the Toyota way, university senior management canvassed the country on a genchi genbutsu *visit to the leading corporate universities. They weren't impressed with what they found. They saw little more than classes and catalogs. They didn't find what they were looking for: an integrated effort focused on creating intellectual capital and building deep discipline around solving real-world business problems. They found few corporate universities acting as a primary resource on performance improvement. Few had the ear of senior management on strategic issues. Some were better than others, yet nearly every organization held the perspective that the corporate university structure was, at the end of the day, "the training folks."*

University management wanted nothing to do with that model. They needed a model that leveraged the way mastery was built in the production environment: managers as models, mentors and monitors, and learning by doing. They needed a model that was every bit a knowledge supply chain designed with the same expertise used to construct

Toyota's vehicle- and parts-supply chains. That knowledge supply chain needed to be managed like any other value stream: Information and expertise needed to flow like parts down an assembly line in the Toyota Production System—just enough delivered just in time with just the right quality. Above all, they needed a model that added value by moving the business forward in a way more akin to an expert advisory counsel than an academic institution.

It had to be about learning, not education. "Catalogs and courseware" wasn't the right model. It didn't fit. It wouldn't work at Toyota. It had to be disciplinary, not programmatic.

The challenge became building a shared understanding of that vision and designing both a workable system as well as a clear development approach.

To galvanize university staff into collectively creating and owning a picture of the desired future, a fictitious obituary was drafted. Entitled "The University of Toyota Calls It Quits, A Requiem for a Noble Concept," the article detailed the path to failure. Constructed as an exposé set three years in the future, it described a corporate university that was everything management didn't want the University of Toyota to be. It worked. The university team clarified the single issue that would be their demise: simple failure to align itself around the real business needs of the organization.

The article was a call to arms, and set the imaginative wheels in motion. The group redrafted the article to be not an obituary, but a front page story trumpeting the success of the university. The group painted a vivid picture of the future, a picture that emerged looking less like traditional corporate education than anyone had anticipated. They surprised themselves. There was nothing conventional or intuitive about that picture.

The image was not a school. It was a practice, developed around helping the organization get things done. There would be no money spent on catalogs or any other typical trappings of a corporate university. There would be no march down the old and beaten training path. It was not about programs, but about performance.

In fact, they didn't see themselves as a corporate university in the traditional sense of the word. The goal was not to promote education, but to transfer real working knowledge.

A unified strategy with three targets emerged: personal mastery, operational excellence, and customer focus. The direction was set. The targets were well aligned to the guiding principles of the organization. The task now became one of designing the structure and developmental approach. It had to be lean.

Education would be embedded into a program of helping to move the business forward. Learning would be delivered as needed by the customer, not through a set course schedule. Complexity in the form of overdesigned courses and waste in the form of extraneous programs was to be avoided at all costs. Close relationships had to be built with each division in order to understand the customer's business needs. That required a structural tie to the business units through dedicated university liaisons embedded in the unit itself. It was just enough structure. It was full-time genchi genbutsu.

During 1999, the Toyota way was codified to embrace two core values: Continuous Improvement and Respect for People. The timing was perfect. It made sense to build practices around those themes, rather than specific job functions.

For example, under the heading of Continuous Improvement came two signature programs. One was devoted to instilling the Kaizen ethic at both team and individual levels. Teams tackled real-world problems that were diagnosed, solved, and implemented by the team. Each idea was tracked through documentation capturing gains from cost savings and improved productivity. The other was devoted to building managers' coaching skills, designed around the model used in the production setting and focused on teasing out strengths of individuals to match talent to task. The goal was engagement.

By keeping it lean, they kept it real. To this day, the University of Toyota does not have a catalog. Because at the end of the day, courses and catalogs do not a university make.

Get Well Sooner

MinuteClinic Takes the Complexity Out of Health Care

Health care is supposed to be a complex issue. Not for MinuteClinic. While others wait hours in urgent care and emergency rooms for even minor ailments, MinuteClinic gets you in and out in 15 minutes. It's Jiffy-Lube for the flu. That's a big problem solved, in a very lean and elegant way.

With a tagline of "You're Sick, We're Quick," the concept is powerfully simple. A nurse practitioner qualified to treat the most common illnesses runs the show. Those illnesses appear on a menu—if it's not on the menu, it doesn't get treated. No appointment is needed. No treatment takes more than 15 minutes. Overhead is low due to the small footprint and absence of medical equipment. Most MinuteClinics are located in a large retail store like Target, so time wasted waiting is minimized: Patients just grab a pager and go shopping while they wait to get beeped when it's their turn.

Customer satisfaction is near 100%. The value proposition is clear and compelling: quick, affordable treatment. Funny, that's exactly opposite of what most hospitals offer.

LeapFrog: Simplicity the Smart Way

Advice from Technologists: Rein in Technology.

For most technology-based firms, more is better. The temptation for technologists is to get too clever. Which usually means more bells, whistles, lights, and screens. In essence, more complexity. According to LeapFrog, the educational technology company, that's all wrong. Technology must always be in service to the idea.

And for LeapFrog, the goal is changing how kids learn to read. With their paper-based multimedia technology products featuring an electronic pen-based system, children touch the stylus to words in a book that rests upon a plastic pad fitted with tiny circuits that emit radio-frequency signals that radiate through the paper. As the stylus is dragged over words, software reads the text through a small built-in speaker.

But for LeapFrog, it's not about technology. It's about solving problems. Technology is always subordinate to the goal of engaging children in a rich learning experience. For LeapFrog, the technology must be invisible. Otherwise, it gets in the way of the mission. If they catch a whiff of technology, they head back to the drawing board.

Zeroing in on Lean

Zero inventory. Zero confusion. THAT'S lean.

Dell has accomplished what no other manufacturer has: zero inventory. That means no warehouses. None. Not even Toyota can touch that. In fact, inventory remains the root of all evil in American automotive retailing.

It's a sin at Dell as well. So much so that they view inventory as ignorance, a hedge against poor demand forecasting and poor ability to see into the supply chain. That's a mindshift from the conventional wisdom that views slack resources, inventory, and order backlog as some kind of operational security blanket. Dell's approach is counterintuitive, a sure sign they're thinking lean.

Dell builds nearly 80,000 PCs a day. Yet at no point in the process does it carry more than two hours of inventory. To do that, you must keep your processes lean. In fact, Dell carries a maximum of three days' supply across its entire chain. Contrast that to their operations in the mid-1990s, when they carried a three-week supply in a vast array of warehouses. And compare it to competitor Hewlett-Packard, which keeps a six-week supply. Dell turns its inventory over 100 times a year. HP, under nine. Obviously a faster inventory turn rate means lower costs. In a business like computers or cars, that's a huge advantage. It gives velocity to your capital, which the Wall Street gurus call "free cash flow."

Like Toyota, Dell views reducing the waste of inventory to be like draining a lake. All the rocks are seen. The problems are more easily revealed, so they can be more quickly solved.

At the **Toyota** plant in Kentucky, a Camry is produced every 58 seconds. Until recently, an hourly team member on the assembly line had nine kinds of seat belts and twenty-four kinds of visors to choose from. That meant too many decisions to make per car. And complexity is the enemy.

The goal: reduce the number of total decisions to a maximum of two per vehicle. Scale it back. Make it simple. Let it flow.

Traditional thinking would limit the options on visors and seat belts. But in a truly elegant solution, the same team member now simply gets parts for each car in a small plastic container holding seat belts and visors perfectly matched to the vehicle arriving at the operator's station.

The result is zero decisions, which in turn dramatically reduces the mental burden on team members. Complexity banished, elegance accomplished.

TOOLKIT: COMPLEXITY MAP

What does complexity look like in your world? Use the following grid to examine your products, services, and processes through the lens of the customer. A customer is defined as any entity in direct receipt of what you, your team, or your company provides.

Then declare war on complexity. And conquer it.

Product/Service/Process_____

Element of Complexity	Characteristic
INCONSISTENCY *Inconsistency destroys reliability and predictability.*	• **Irregularity** • **Interruption** • **Imbalance**
OVERLOAD *Overload limits productivity, functionality, and effectiveness.*	• **Stress, strain, push** • **Undercapacity** • **Overburden**
WASTE *Waste is elegance enemy number one. Excess beyond what's absolutely needed to solve the problem is considered waste. Too much or too many of anything consumes resources without adding any value. Customers won't pay for it. Translate each of these deadly sins to your business.* *For example, overcapacity might mean excess floor space in retail operations.*	• **Overcapacity** • **Overdesign** • **Excess motion** • **Defects** • **Bureaucracy** • **Overprocess** • **Delay** • **Inventory** • **Overproduction** • **Transport** • **Redundancy**

HANSEI

How easy is it for customers to pull value from you?

How well does value flow to customers?

What would your customers love for you to eliminate?

How do inconsistency, overload, and waste impact your operation?

Which key processes are designed from the customer back?

PROTOCOL FOR PRACTICES

We've now covered the three principles and ten practices that guide the journey toward elegant solutions. The diagram below should serve to provide a visual memory jogger.

The question now becomes: *How do I get started putting these ideas into action in a practical way?* Part 3 provides the answer.

TOYOTA'S FORMULA FOR MASTERING INNOVATION

The Tyranny of Complexity

The high cost of complexity is staggering. Like poor quality, we put up with it as consumers. We shrug our shoulders at the fact that we waste an exorbitant amount of time in queues at airports, movie theaters, post offices, and restaurants. We tolerate any number of other aggravations: searching for what we want at the big-box stores; opening a package of D-cell batteries; unwrapping a CD; navigating an overdesigned Web site; making it through the maze of whatever automated voicemail system we're up against.

> *What's up with packaging? Batteries they protect like gold. You can never open those things. But lightbulbs...???*
> **Ellen DeGeneres**

Unfortunately, we let our apathy creep into our business operations. Into our design of products, services, and systems. And that's unforgivable. If you hate complexity as a consumer, you should absolutely detest it as a producer.

We lament the speed of change, yet we continue to build systems and structures that slow our response to the rapidly changing requirements of a demanding marketplace, often confusing customization with complexity. The high cost of complexity will stop you dead in your tracks. Gone unheeded, it will eventually destroy whatever value you do provide.

So start looking at the world through the eyes of the user. Start listening to the front line, because they know best what's stupid. Start fixing things if they're broken.

Most important, stop increasing complexity. Stop adding stuff no one really needs. Stop making things more complicated than they need to be. Stop making it difficult. Stop overloading. Stop wasting valuable resources—yours and those of others.

When it comes to innovation and designing solutions, whatever you do, keep it lean. Scale it back, make it simple, and let it flow.

That's what elegance is all about.

3
part

protocol
p's and q's

CHAPTER 14

The Clamshell Strategy

The beginning is the chiefest part of any work.

Plato

Preparing the Leadership

"I can't get my ideas heard."

"We've tried things like this before, they got shot down."

"I've suggested several improvements, but nothing came of it."

"We have these great offsites where we come home raring to go with an action plan to change the world. But we never do."

"Our culture is command and control. Forget creativity."

Sound familiar? It's the sound of silence. Idea silence. Somehow we've pigeonholed creativity into belonging to the so-called "creatives" in design, marketing, advertising, and R&D. Or to the big shots in the organization who can handle the big ideas. But they're not any more creative than the next person, their jobs are just different.

Innovation must occur at every level of the company. We all know that. But that doesn't necessarily mean administrative assistants are going to create your next breakthrough product. It does mean they must find a way to do something within their control better than it's ever been done before. Every day.

Once you understand that the net impact of innovation is relative to one's base of responsibility, power, and control, you begin to see the potential of 360° innovation. As you move up the ladder, you get more of all three, so your innovation quotient rises.

But think about this: If innovation is everyone's job, where does the greatest cumulative potential reside? With the lower levels. It's a numbers game. There are more of us down on the front lines, more of us working with the system every day, more of us serving customers daily.

So the challenge is how to draw out the creative power of people in an organized, systematic way that provides a safe haven for everyone involved and begins to embed a real discipline around finding and solving problems. That's Toyota's real magic.

Here's how you can tap into it in your organization.

Getting Started

It all starts with a single team—one manager and a team of up to ten direct reports. Let's say that manager is you. The strategy is the same whether you're CEO or a first-rung supervisor, but know that change spreads and happens faster at the front lines.

You now strike a deal up front. The Japanese call it *nemawashi* (nim-ah-wash-ee), a word drawn from the practice of bonzai, and which means "preparing to plant." It's blatantly but constructively political. You agree to sanction your team's idea or solution, one they choose, if it meets the right criteria:

(1) the team works in the general territory of something you feel needs attention—something of concern or that clearly advances a current objective;

(2) the idea theme must concern something within your base of responsibility, power, and control;

(3) the team arrives at a no- or low-cost solution that can be piloted quickly, within thirty days;

(4) the team works on a problem they all touch, using a systematic problem-solving methodology;

(5) the project must result in a clear value enhancement: quality, cost, speed, etc.;

(6) the project is an experiment, and nothing gets broad execution until the learning is captured and there's a compelling case for feeding it forward.

You've now guaranteed idea acceptance, built the necessary accountability, and released the collective energy of individuals to create and innovate without hesitancy, fear of failure, or any of the myriad other barriers that typically present obstacles to innovation. It nicely avoids the three temptations (swinging for fences, et al.) covered in Chapter 1.

It's a *clamshell strategy*: you provide the necessary air cover and support from the top, the team does the heavy lifting from the bottom. And a pearl of innovation results. You're on your way. Let's take a closer look.

STOP!

Yes, it all sounds too pat, too easy. Okay, so there are a few caveats. Three things you absolutely cannot do. For the good managers out there, these are nonissues. For the rest, these are the three things you must not do.

1. Don't be bossy. There's a time and place for barking orders. When you're asking for innovative ideas and solutions isn't one of them. Managing innovation is like conducting a controlled burn. Too much control, and the fire has to be restarted, over and over again.

2. Don't hoard information. There's a time and place for the "need to know" basis of disseminating information. When you're sending people to solve important problems isn't one of them. Anything less than full transparency limits the team's power and effectiveness.

3. Don't change direction. There's a time and place for shifting priorities. Midstream in the pursuit of key opportunities isn't one of them. Clarity and constancy to purpose goes a long way toward creating the kind of innovation religion you want.

Your job is to tap and guide the ingenuity of your team. Being bossy, hoarding information, and changing direction will stop you dead in your tracks. Because all three erode trust. No trust, no commitment. No commitment, no ideas…innovation D.O.A.!

Micromanaging innovation is like trying to rope the wind. It's self-defeating and pointless. You'll exhaust your energy and stifle your team, while all the great ideas floating on the winds of change remain at large. Managing innovation well requires a fine balance between letting go and reining in. There are three things you need to do. Or start doing.

Start!

If you're struggling to build a constantly innovating team, you may need to rethink your role as a manager. The term itself has too much baggage weighing it down. Instead, start thinking about yourself more as a chief design engineer, a grand master of elegant innovation, guiding a team of business designers, artists, scientists, and engineers.

The Pledge:

I promise to release my team to find a better way.

At Toyota, the chief engineer mindset lives at all levels, not just with the individual talented, experienced, and wise enough to actually carry the title. The role is a special one. It's not an easy one to fill. There are three dimensions, three hats you must wear.

Model. That means mastering innovation at the personal level as discussed in Chapter 1, *The Art of Ingenuity.* Full engagement and exploration is the call: constantly reinventing your own work, challenging yourself, and managing your individual ideas. You should be a team member of a higher-level team. Modeling innovation is one of the most powerful ways to influence others.

Mentor. Chief engineers *ask* for innovation. They commission it. View yourself as an investor in the stock trade of the team: ideas. Guidance comes in the form of coaching and teaching in a mostly Socratic way: challenging the thinking, asking questions to enable team members to arrive at their own insight.

Your Choice:

If the idea of chief design engineer doesn't quite resonate with you, or you can't bring yourself to drop the manager idea, then try this: portfolio manager. Either way, the charge is the same—guiding a full repertoire of ideas and projects aimed at reinventing the work, solving important problems, and pursuing the proper opportunities.

Monitor. Without clear metrics specific to innovation, proper attention won't get paid. How many ideas per week do you want from each individual? How many team projects do you want in your portfolio? What percent of time is devoted to *improving* the work, not just *doing* the work?

To make it real, make it metric!

GOT GAME?

You know your role. Now you have to define the playing field, pick the team, and rally it to execute the game plan.

> *To be an innovative company, you have to ask for innovation. You assemble a group of talented people who are eager to do new things and put them in an environment where innovation is expected. It's that simple, and that hard.*
>
> **Paul Cook**

The Field

If you keep the *pursuit of perfection* principle in mind, it shouldn't be too hard to bracket the territory the team needs to tackle, study, and innovate around. Your job is not to pick the specific target, problem, or project, but rather to point them in the direction of priority, meaning the goals and objectives intended to create value for those directly consuming what your group produces on a daily basis. In other words, your customers.

Your playing field is the whole of the work that your area contributes to the larger system. The focus of the team should be on some lesser part of the whole. A subordinate theme.

And specifically where do you start? Well, what's the most important part of a car? It's the part that's not working. So start there. I'm betting you have a pretty good sense of what keeps you up at night. Point your team in that direction.

But...

Don't address a target where there is no consensus on the issue's importance to the company or customers. *Don't* head for an area lacking good visibility. *Don't* work on something where results won't show up for months. *Don't* pick a target fraught with controversy. *Don't* select themes lacking strong interest. *Don't* select something beyond the control of the team. *Don't* target an issue already undergoing study or change. *Don't* use this as an opportunity to execute an already developed solution.

And *don't* head for anything that isn't part of the daily work.

The Team

Who you pick is as important as what you pick. So pick your best job-diggers. The ones that best exemplify the principle of *ingenuity in craft*. The key quality is keen interest.

Beyond that, each team member should have subject matter knowledge, if not expertise. They should represent a key touch point to the process being examined, and work closely with some functional aspect of the theme. Make sure they are responsible and play well with others.

Perspective:

Much of the energy invested in change efforts by U.S. organizations has nothing to do with innovation or real improvement. The truth is that many "ideas don't get heard" because they aren't legitimate ideas. They're thinly veiled attempts to advance one's career by expanding a base of power and control over resources. They're in the best interest of the individual, not the team, department, manager, or organization. Most important, they add no value for customers.

Cause: The new person does things differently than the old person, and wants to make a mark before they move on. Change is made, without company goals being directly advanced. But the individual's résumé is.

Cure: Work within the current base of power and control. Exhaust it. Improve your work within the limits.

And for the larger ideas, problems, and opportunities, tackle them as a team.

And take a lesson from Malcolm Gladwell's *The Tipping Point.* Since you need to look beyond the first team's project to the day where constant innovation is a way of life, you need to work toward building a critical mass. You need things to *tip*. How? By leveraging the few key players who can make it happen.

The *Connectors,* who will get the word out about the team's success through their well-developed social networks.

The *Mavens,* who will dig deeper than the others to become experts in the team-based innovation process.

The *Salesmen,* who will use their inherent powers of persuasion to convince and motivate any fence sitters or doubting Thomases.

The Plan

Two simple tactics can help you launch your first team.

First is the *team captain*—a team member likely of the *Maven* ilk, who will act as the key contact point for all communication and documentation. The captain fully participates in the work of the team, but has the additional responsibility of coordination. Meeting schedules, agendas, data, and documents are all part of the captain's role. The captain acts as your main source of information on the team's progress.

Second is the *straight talk*—the pre-game

rallying message, as it were. The two big questions on their mind will be: *Why am I here?* and *What is the objective?* So this is where you provide context, issue the challenge, and convey the importance of the team. This is where you talk about the importance of ingenuity, perfection, and the connection to customers.

> Leaders rally people to a better future.
> **Marcus Buckingham**

This is where you talk about the gap between today and tomorrow, as you see it. This is where you tell them how we got here, and why they have been chosen. This is where you tell them the scope and direction of where you'd like them to exert their best thinking. This is where you reinforce that you have no preconceived solutions, that the specific problem addressed or project chosen is up to them, but that you're looking for a low- or no-cost solution.

This is where you tell them that gaining depth in the team problem-solving discipline and techniques is as important as the outcome. This is where you tell them they will execute their own solution. This is where you show your appreciation in advance for the hard work.

And it's where you tell them you look forward to hearing their elegant solution.

Avoiding Abilene

Teams unaccustomed to working together are vulnerable to "groupthink," aka inability to be provocative in the face of, and thus manage, unwilling agreement. Author Jerry Harvey describes the dynamic in his story *The Abilene Paradox.* No one really wants to go to Abilene, but someone suggests it. The entire group ends up there, because no one wants to rock the boat, dissent, contradict, or offend anyone.

Ever been? It happens *all the time!* If it happens to your team, you can forget about the elegant solution. Try *Abilene* solution.

The key to avoiding *Abilene* is understanding that team-based innovation is not about team-building. It's not about social

> Toto, I've a feeling we're not in Kansas anymore!
> **Judy Garland as Dorothy**
> *The Wizard of Oz*

skills and interpersonal relationships; it's about social engineering. It's about building a deep discipline around collectively solving problems. That's very, very hard. It's relatively alien to most. We don't get schooled in it.

Two key tools can help. One you already know. The other is readily available. First is the IDEA Loop. *Investigate—Design—Execute—Adjust.* Use it as the central standard tool. Follow it. Leverage it fully. How you execute the process will depend on the team, but complete each phase thoroughly before moving to the next.

Second is the *outside expert*—an objective individual from inside or outside the company trained in team problem-solving methods and group facilitation who will work with you and the team to instill the required discipline. The outside expert has no skin in the game other than ensuring proper process. Your team will actually learn better and progress faster, because the outsider can see obstacles like bias and groupthink clearly, and is trained to constructively and productively move the group beyond them.

Exploit both tools fully, and you'll avoid the Abilene solution.

How to Fail

The Clamshell Strategy, like any strategy, requires leadership to be successful. And while that grand topic is far beyond the bounds of this treatment, it's worth a brief visit. Because the lack of leaders and leadership at every level will derail even your best-laid plans.

Of all the definitions of leadership in the world, the one most appropriate and accessible to the everyman is the one offered by John Seely Brown, of Xerox's Palo Alto Research Center fame,

Toyota on Leadership

Former Toyota senior managing director Masao Nemoto had ten guiding principles of leadership, known to associates as "Nemoto's Sayings." Nemoto developed these principles in an effort to minimize the negative impact of personal management styles inhibiting team performance.

1. Improvement after improvement.

2. Coordinate between divisions.

3. Everyone speaks.

4. Do not scold.

5. Ensure others understand your work.

6. Send the best associates out for rotation.

7. A command without a deadline is not a command.

8. Rehearsal is an ideal occasion for training.

9. Inspection is a failure if top management takes no action.

10. Ask subordinates, "What can I do for you?"

who maintains that *"leaders make meaning."* That simple definition is on the money. Great innovation has a lot in common with great leadership.

The innovative leader needs three basic qualities.

Integrity, which comes from consistently accepting responsibility and demonstrating sound judgment, defined as doing the right thing.

Vision, which comes from a well-anchored ambition set firmly toward creating a new reality all can share.

Guidance, which comes from a sincere desire to see people succeed, demonstrated through unwavering support and constant encouragement.

SO. It's fairly easy to see how any dream of creating and developing a strong group capability around innovation can go up in smoke. In fact, you can do it in three easy steps.

Don't commit fully—without full conviction, you'll garner none.

Micromanage the effort—think air cover, not troop inspection.

Delegate your accountability—deny ownership, and it all falls apart.

A glance at the daily business news headlines reveals why failure is so abundant in our organizations.

> Better thinking in an organization is not a matter of smart hiring, it is a matter of setting up the processes and systems...to encourage people to think, and allow that thinking to be used.
> **Thomas Stewart**

HANSEI

> *What about your area of work most keeps you up at night?*
> *What processes, problems, and projects can your team tackle?*
> *What opportunities seem best suited to a team approach?*
> *What should the makeup of the team be?*
> *How will you provide the necessary support and guidance?*

CHAPTER 15

The Elegant Solution

There are risks and costs to a program of action. But they are far less than
the long-range risks and costs of comfortable inaction.

John F. Kennedy

Diary of an Idea

*Can a group that has never had any exposure to this kind of thinking
and that has never worked together as a team pool their energy in a
focused way to discover an elegant solution and find a way to do
something better than it's ever been done before?*

*Can an inexperienced frontline team put the practices into play to
effectively solve a real-world problem? Innovate?*

*Is it even possible to learn collaborative design and apply the principles
and practices of innovation in a single sitting?*

Yes. But you have to commit. You have to dig in and just do it.

The Los Angeles Police Department (LAPD) began working with
the University of Toyota midway through 2005. Following a number of
exploratory meetings with LAPD's command staff, the university and
its team of masters decided to assist LAPD in *pro bono* fashion. It was a
partnership that made sense. It would be a challenging experiment. It
would test whether Toyota's principles and practices could travel
beyond Toyota and the automotive world. It would test those
techniques in a nonproduction environment. In fact, it would test them
in a non-business environment. It represented an important social contribution to a critical community service in desperate need of
improvement.

It was the right thing to do. And we would learn.

Initiative leaders were briefed in the fashion described in the previous chapter. Four pilot teams were selected. Three from the Jail Division. One from the Professional Standards Bureau, which was home to Internal Affairs. The Jail Division needed breakthroughs in the booking process. Professional Standards wanted to look at their entire operation from a new perspective.

Following a brief overview to the Toyota approach, three teams went to work. That's the Toyota way: *application comes first.*

This is the diary of one team's journey to the elegant solution.

8:00 a.m.

We're gathered together, eight plus me, to solve a wicked problem facing the City of Los Angeles. The team before me is from the Jail Division of the Los Angeles Police Department. They represent eight different functions and three different jails. They've never worked together as a team. In fact, only two people know each other. It's not ideal, because they're not a natural work group. But you can't shut an entire jail down.

> City government has had the reputation of, OK, it doesn't matter how much you waste. You have to get away from that.
> **Capt. Patrick Findley**
> Los Angeles Police Department

From my perspective, it's going to be a long and difficult day. My colleagues, the other Toyota masters who are with me to coach the other teams, feel the same way. This is untested territory. We're out of our comfort zone. But that's a good thing. It means we'll learn. And that's the ultimate goal for today. Regardless of outcome, we'll be smarter by the end of the day. We'll know whether our hypothesis is valid. We'll know one way or the other if our brand of innovative thinking is transportable.

We've just heard the commanding officer of the Division, Captain Patrick Findley, a direct report to LAPD Chief William Bratton, lay out the challenge: *"Our booking process is broken. It keeps me up at night. We need officers out on the street, not stuck in paperwork acting as arrestee escorts. I want you to render the way we do things now obsolete. Give me your best ideas, and a plan. I'll be back with other members of the command staff to hear from you at 3 p.m."* And with that, we're off to the races.

8:30 a.m.—5 hours left

Report at 3 means stop at 2:30. Five hours plus lunch. No easy challenge. They've never done any organized problem solving.

My charge? I'm the guide on the side. I need to play the role of muse. Draw out the creativity. Challenge their thinking. Lead them to their own conclusions and insights. Educate while doing—they must learn to think differently, and apply that thinking immediately. Learn the way on the way. They have the solution, not me. They know the work, I don't. But I don't need to. I know how to get them to the idea, whatever it is they wish to chase.

Introductions all around. It's like pulling teeth. The heads are down. Apprehension hangs heavy. Name and title is about all I get. Working in a jail obviously takes its toll on a person, or perhaps it's just the bureaucracy of civil service.

How do I break the ice? I need to connect quickly. Each will have a role in the process as the day unfolds. A leader will emerge. A naysayer will emerge. And everything in between. I will need to rechannel all eight forms of personal energy toward solving a problem. I need to know who and what I'm working with.

"If you were a part of a car, what would it be?" I ask. Signs of life. Good! Some very creative answers: Muffler. Sunroof. Seat belt. Glove box. *"What's the most important part?"* I challenge. Typical answers: Their part. No single part. *"Think differently,"* I prod. Silence. *"It's the part that's not working."* They're digesting that.

It worked. Lightbulbs. Smiles. Now they're awake. Now the floodgates. *"What do they want from us?"* *"Is this all about money?"* *"You ever worked in city government before?"* *"We've had plenty ideas. No one listens. Nothing will come of this."*

Venting is good. I assure them their ideas will not only be heard, but if thought well through, accepted and sanctioned. They're skeptical. But they bite.

8:45 a.m.

The first thing we need to do is bracket things. We're looking at the booking process. We need cops on the street, not inside, that much we know. But we need to draw it out, to *think in pictures*.

So we have a little fun. First assignment: a little strategic graffiti. Big paper. Sticky notes on steroids put together in a five-panel mural. I don't want a process map. I don't want a fishbone diagram. We'll get there in a bit. I want the right brain to kick in. I want a sketch. I don't care if it's stick figures. *Show* me what it's like to work in a jail, booking criminals. Draw me a picture of who's involved. How do they feel? What works, what doesn't. What's a day in the life look like? And make it vibrant!

> *Any technique which will increase self-knowledge in depth should in principle increase one's creativity.*
> **Abraham Maslow**

No one jumps up, so I start the picture smack dab in the middle with a prisoner behind bars and a half angry, half sad face. That gets the juices flowing.

Inside fifteen minutes we have imagery, we have color. We have a shared physical, emotional, and mental map of what's going on. The booking process is definitely a sick patient. Officers with rain clouds over their heads, legs shackled to dozens of piles of papers that bookers can't see over. Arrestees queued up all around the perimeter. *Help!* scribbled all over. Management portrayed by the *see no evil, hear no evil, speak no evil* triad.

They're defrosting, coming out of their shells. The dirty laundry is being aired, but in a productive way. Ingenuity must be invoked. But that won't happen unless we drop the baggage. It's a good start. Minds and eyes are opening. It's time for the more structured stuff.

10:30 a.m.—3 hours left

We've spent a better part of the morning grasping the situation, trying to nail down the current reality in a tangible way. In order to *learn to see* the situation for what it really is, the team must invoke their power of observation, if only virtually.

We're after details. We're sweating the small stuff. Team members have called back to their operations to get forms and reports faxed over.

They've called officers to get the voice of the customer in the room. They've checked regulations.

This is hard for them. They want action, not thought. But that's part of the discipline. They remark that they've never thought this hard about anything. They've never examined anything so excrutiatingly.

What's stupid about it? Why does it take so long? One thing we know for sure: It's convoluted and complex. What's fascinating is that there are eight different versions of the whole mess.

It's tough to separate the *as is* from the *should be*. We need an aerial perspective. I teach them simple process mapping, nothing complicated. A basic tool to validate what's going on and provide a visual model of the current process. As they begin to map it out, clarity improves. Consensus is facilitated. The macro steps come into view.

Officer arrives with arrestee. Required forms are completed and stamped. Females and males are searched and wanded in different jail blocks. In cases of contraband, weapons, or violent arrests, strip searches are conducted. If medical treatment is necessary, the officer escorts the arrestee to the dispensary.

When all that's done, the officer finally arrives at the booking window. The booker reviews paperwork; booking starts. Property and money is itemized and enveloped. Wristbands are placed on the arrestee, who is then carted off to a holding cell. Officers collect their required paperwork and depart.

The whole thing could take up to three hours.

They're shaking their heads. It's taken us ninety minutes just to agree on what actually happens. And we haven't even defined the real problem yet.

12 noon—2.5 hours left

They're getting tense. Truth be told, I'm a little worried. We need to work through lunch, gain another hour. Another ninety minutes won't cut it. Not at this rate. We have to *master the tension.*

They want to leap to solutions. *We should do X. We really need to do Y.*

I won't let them. Not completely. Most of my energy is spent reining them in. Leaping is natural, instinctive. But wrong.

We need to agree on the problem first. Until we do, we can't even begin to solve it. We have the major symptom: *delay*. We need the differential diagnosis. I show them how to use a fishbone diagram to chart out the situation we've described to help us get a bead on the primary contributing causes. We need tight scope and laserlike focus. No need to scrap the whole thing. I relate the story of logjams.

> *To restore flow to the river, logjams used to be simply blown up with dynamite. Valuable lumber was lost, and it didn't always work. Finally someone got the notion to go up in a helicopter and look down on the problem. Turns out a single log tangled sideways was to blame. Solution? Lift the log out, flow restored.*

Fishboning helps pinpoint the primary offender by giving you an elevated perspective. It's an age-old and widely used technique, but effective. Finally, a breakthrough. Maybe they needed sugar.

Here it is: The medical treatment step, if and when needed, creates a huge delay in the whole process. It can keep cops off the street for at least two hours. Now they can frame the problem properly:

> *If medical treatment of an arrestee is required, they must be transported to the larger regional jail facilities before booking, resulting in excessive wait time and redundant transport time for the arresting officer.*

Now we have something to solve.

1:00 p.m.—90 minutes left

Things are starting to click. We even have time for a quick breather. Next up: the diagnosis.

Why the delay due to medical treatment? Current protocol doesn't allow booking at a smaller outlying jail if medical treatment is required. Root cause? Blanket policy dictates that when arrestees claim any kind of medical condition, they have to be transported to a regional facility first to be examined, then back to the outlying jail for booking. Half the time it's minor, like a scrape, cut, or bruise. Luckily, a nurse is on the team to lend the voice of experience: 45 minutes is the average wait time.

We *run the numbers*. Forty percent of the average 3000 bookings per smaller outlying jail that currently involve a medical treatment step don't really require it, because they're nonemergencies. No doctor needed! Arrestees use it to stall. Squad cars operate at $300 per hour. That's costing one jail alone over $3 million a year. Multiply that by a dozen city jails, and it starts to become staggering. And we don't even bother trying to compute the impairment to crime fighting.

The need is clear and present. The potential social impact is significant. Saving that 45 minutes will increase productivity, reduce officer stress, provide better community service, reduce liability. It will achieve the Division goals of more field time for officers. It will make L.A.'s part of the world a nicer place to be.

Time to move into design mode. *Design for today.* Solve it now. Draw it out, think in pictures: what do we really want? What's the perfect booking look like from the customer's perspective? Answer: Drop and go. Don't even set foot in the jail. Like a video drop box.

That's the ideal. That's what we need to aim for. We know we can't do that in a month. Too much for this team to do alone.

How do we *leverage the limits? What can we do? What is possible? What is needed?* The dance begins.

2:00 p.m.—30 minutes and counting

The target is set: Eliminate 50% of the current booking time. Increase throughput 40%. That's a stretch. And the goals conflict. Good. They can't be achieved by just working harder. *Keeping it lean* means no new resources allowed. Can't add heads. Can't build out the jail. Or build a new one.

We need innovative thinking.

Finally we're right where they wanted to be three hours ago. Brainstorming. Funny thing is, now that we've dug deep into the problem, all the ideas floated earlier have no applicability.

The solution seems so clear, so simple:

Book first at the outlying jails in stable, minor, or nonemergency medical situations.

It's a no-brainer in retrospect, but it took all day to see it. Simply modify one step of the process. Eliminate the delay entirely. That's time better spent on the street. Booking time goes down, throughput goes up.

They've done it. They've created a new standard. And that's the basis for kaizen. We spend time thinking through the effects on the system, all the likely challenges and possible pushback.

The plan of action comes easily. They'll run a test for a month—one deployment period—at one jail. Then they will compare the pilot jail to the others, the controls. I didn't even have to tell them that. They're getting it. It's all an experiment. *Let learning lead.* If it works, fantastic. We can launch it big. Go citywide. If it doesn't, they'll learn why. And the seeds of kaizen have been planted.

It's 2:30. Time to prepare for the presentation to Command.

3 p.m.—Showtime

As we enter the presentation room, we stop dead in our tracks. We expected the captain to be there. Perhaps a few others. We're face-to-face with two tables occupied by the central command staff of the Los Angeles Police Department. Ten senior ranking officials. Chief Bratton's right-hand man, Assistant Chief Gascon, is there. He's flanked by commanders from various divisions and departments. No one expected this. I sure didn't.

Meanwhile...

The other teams define the problem differently, and arrive at different solutions.

One team sees a problem when unannounced special task force "sweeps" overload the process, and creates a standard "Special Team" system to handle it, using the quickest and best bookers and a modified workflow.

Another sees the problem originating in the field, and designs a simple "Pack 'n' Go" kit for officers in squad cars to enable them to save time by preparing booking papers in advance on the way to the jail.

But you couldn't wish for a better audience. The teams almost certainly have never met any of these leaders before. What an opportunity. I recall the comments that *our ideas never get heard.* They will now.

They're nervous. They have every right to be. They've never done any public speaking. This is all brand new. It will be one of the most powerful learning experiences they will ever have. They have to just do it. And they do. Each team in turn presents in their ten-minute window. They field the challenges with aplomb. The teams all support one another. The camaraderie is palpable.

> Today, changes must come fast; and we must adjust our mental habits, so that we can accept comfortably the idea of stopping one thing and beginning another overnight.
>
> **Donald M. Nelson**

There's a moment of silence at the end. Chief Gascon stands. His voice is tinged with emotion. He is clearly thunderstruck.

"This...is...huge. I'm floored by your creative thinking. I would have never thought of these things. You've got breakthroughs here. This will save time, save lives, save resources. It supports all of our goals. We will do all of these things. I'm anxious to see the results of the tests. Please keep me informed. Thank you all for your hard work and great teamwork. Thank you for this."

And the elephant in the room? *Why haven't we done this before?*

I know the answers. No discipline to get to the ideas. No formula for mastering innovation and making it a way of life.

HANSEI

What parts of this book seemed to hit home with you?

How do you plan to enact the three principles of innovation?

How can you best use this book to drive change and innovation?

What new ideas do you have after reading this book?

How many ideas will you implement next year?

Words of Encouragement

Security can only be achieved through constant change, through discarding old ideas
that have outlived their usefulness and adapting others to current facts.
William O. Douglas

Elegance Ain't Easy

Innovation is at or near the center of nearly everyone's radar screen. If you're not looking for it in your work, you're looking for it in your avocations. Because stirring in each of us is the desire to employ our creative spirit through what we do every day. At some level, we're all scientists and artists at heart.

The evidence is all around us. It's there in the strategies we concoct, teams we supervise, projects we manage, deals we cut, reports we prepare, and software we program. From the clean edge of the mason's mortar to the impossible marriage of microscopic nerve endings at the hands of the skilled neurosurgeon; from the immaculate order of the sharp-eyed chambermaid to the technical wizardry of the systems engineer; from the cheerful wave of the monthly gas meter-reader to the stirring eloquence of the visionary leader; from an Apple computer to a Starbucks coffee to a Ferrari automobile—if we can think it, build it, or do it, the opportunity exists to find a way to do it better than it's ever been done before.

> *There really is no such thing as art. There are only artists.*
> **E. H. Gombrich**

The potential to innovate our way to an elegant solution is alive and well in everyone.

Actually *doing* it is another matter entirely.

Reality Bites

A study of the great accomplishments in art, industry, and science reveals a story of constant study and hard work. Mozart, Galileo, Rockefeller, Renoir, Plato, Einstein, Shakespeare, Newton—all were innovative geniuses, and all believed in the constant and purposeful application of talent and self toward a worthy end. Investigation into their magnificent achievements reveals a lifelong process of deep reflection, keen observation, and constant betterment. You've now become familiar with *hansei, genchi genbutsu,* and *kaizen*—reflection, observation, continuous improvement—as important tenets of innovation. The ancient Greeks also believed that to become able in any profession, three things were necessary—*nature, study,* and *practice*. And for over twenty-five years the U.S. Army has employed a leadership model of *Be-Know-Do*. In their view, while acquired knowledge and skill (Know and Do) is necessary and valuable, it is perishable because it can quickly become obsolete in today's competitive environment. It is *Be*—talent, purpose, and ambition—that remains the enduring differentiator.

It's the *achievement* that presents so much difficulty. And for all the same reasons that losing weight and maintaining physical fitness does. It requires lifelong vigilance, discipline, and perseverance. And patience, because it takes time.

And that's something in short supply. But in high demand. The innovation equilibrium is out of balance.

> The very greatest things—great thoughts, discoveries, inventions—have usually been nurtured in hardship, often pondered over in sorrow, and at length established with difficulty.
> **Samuel Smiles**

In general, Western cultures are relatively impatient and nearsighted. We're not that willing and eager to trade immediate gratification and short-term gains for the long-range possibilities. And we begrudgingly respond to change, usually waiting for the fabled burning platform to suddenly and mysteriously appear.

As a result the *as is* prevails over the *could be* for far too long.

The journey to elegance along the pathway of innovation is one most don't commit to making. The reasons? It's not easy, it's not quick, and it doesn't guarantee wealth or success. But do me a favor. Don't be a modern day Archimedes, waiting for a lightning bolt of *Eureka!* to hit you in the bathtub. I'm fairly certain the elegant solution won't magically come to you through the mythical happy accident.

Because there's nothing accidental about true innovation.

Slowly I Turned...

All change demands knowledge. *Meaningful* change—*innovation*—demands *profound* knowledge. Some of that I've tried to impart in this book through the wisdom of Toyota.

Like how big change can be achieved through little steps. Toyota has proven that getting a little better daily results in sustainable market leadership. But again, it takes time. There *are* no overnight sensations—great careers and great companies are built painstakingly over time.

> *Slowly I turned...step by step...inch by inch.*
> **Joey Faye**
> Vaudeville actor, *Niagara*

So be patient. And don't let gradual change and innovation become an excuse for not taking any action at all. That's like people who say they only play the lottery when the jackpot is over $20 million. Instinctive, but illogical.

And while we're on the topic of excuses, resist them at all costs. They're too easy. If I had a penny for every time I've heard people tell me *"Those are great ideas and it all makes sense, but we can't do it here,"* and *"We just don't have the time,"* I'd be permanently camped under a Caribbean cabana with a Cuban cigar, clipping coupons. The excuses usually come just when things get a little hard and the daily fires are allowed to rule the day. Look, everyone's busy. But the question is, what are you busy about? Spend all your time in a defensive and reactive posture, and you'll find yourself getting slower and slower. You'll be playing catch-up. When change outpaces you like that, you're done.

Excuses amount to preemptive surrender. That's unacceptable at Toyota. And it sure doesn't sound much like leadership. If you give up before you even start, not only will you never progress, you'll lose whatever advantage you do have to your competitor who views it as a challenge and so offers up the elegant solution. Your customers won't open their wallets to the wafflers and "we-can't-do-its"; they'll spend their money with the problem-solvers.

> *Conditions and events are neither to be fled from nor passively acquiesced in; they are to be utilized and directed.*
>
> **John Dewey**

It's somewhat natural to want change without doing anything differently. Crazy, sure. But more important, it's a death knell in business.

Fighting Nature

Ever wonder why when *we* offer up an idea on how things should change and improve, it's okay? But the ideas of others we resist? It's because it isn't change we're resisting. We're resisting *being* changed. We want ownership and involvement.

That's natural. The point is that we all face the same challenge, no matter what level we're at. We all feel alone in our organizations at one time or another. Like no one is listening. Like we're an outsider looking in. If I know anything, it is that those below you and above you feel the same way.

So what's the answer?

Think big but play it close to the vest. At least at first. Dig your own job. Improve what you have control over. Work on ideas that are visible to those at least two levels above you. Work on ideas that have high impact and result in outcomes others will respect. Slowly build your network, one person at a time. Build the movement, grow the cause. Be persistent. Involve others. Throw knowledge at people: books, articles, videos, experts. When you do have success, share the credit. Be humble. Success often breeds hubris, and with it complacency. Or worse, self-destruction. Resist the urge to protect your status through means other than the innovative ways that got you there.

And apply what you've learned here. My prediction is that if you do, things will start to get better. Then they'll get worse. They did for me. So you'll have to ride it out. It'll go like this: You'll start with all the trappings, throwing the terms and concepts around. You'll apply the tools and techniques in a mostly willy-nilly fashion, grafting them on to your current *modus operandi*. You'll know enough to be dangerous. But since your deeper principles and assumptions haven't changed, you'll wake up one day and realize, like I did, that you don't know anything. That you don't even know what you don't know. That's the *aha* point.

> **If there is no struggle there is no progress.**
> **Frederick Douglass**

That's when the real learning starts. That's when the long journey to innovation as a way of life actually begins. Now that may take a few years in itself. Patience...patience...

Finally, you'll accept the singular guiding insight to innovation: *To find the elegant solution, you must be inelegant.*

The process is messy. So good luck. Keep at it.

And if all else fails, call me.

Notes & Credits

In addition to first-hand knowledge and experience in working with the Toyota organization for nearly a decade, the primary sources for the Toyota-related stories and cases in this book include, but are not limited to, interviews, press releases, speeches, public Web sites, and publications freely provided to the author. These sources include the following:

Toyota: A History of the First 50 Years. Toyota Motor Corporation, 1988.

The Lexus Story. ©2004 Lexus, a Division of Toyota Motor Sales, U.S.A., Inc. Produced by Melcher Media Inc.

Lexus Case Study: Challenge of the U.S. Luxury Car Market. Toyota Motor Corporation, Overseas Marketing Division and Hitotsubashi University Graduate School of International Corporate Strategy, ©2002, rev. 2004.

The Prius That Shook the World—How Toyota Developed the World's First Mass Production Hybrid Vehicle. Original text by Hideshi Itazoki. Translated by Albert Yamada and Masako Ishikawa. Tokyo, Japan: The Nikkan Kogyo Shimbun, Ltd., 1999.

Scion: Redefining the Customer Experience. Best Practice Bulletin Volume 26. Published by the Global Knowledge Center, Toyota Motor Sales, U.S.A., Inc., April, 2005.

Stretch! The Power of Setting Monumental Goals. How to Save $100 Million in Three Years. A NAPO Toyota Way Case Study. Written by Matthew May for Jane Beseda and Thor Oxnard. 2003.

Dig Your Own Job. A NAPO Toyota Way Case Study, 2003.

Toyota Case Study #1: N.U.M.M.I. Toyota Motor Corporation, October 1999.

Toyota Case Study #6: LS 400 Development. Toyota Motor Corporation, October 1999.

Toyota Case Study #7: Lexus Franchise in the U.S. Toyota Motor Corporation, October 1999.

The Toyota Way 2001. ©2000 Toyota Motor Corporation.

Lexus Magazine. Published by Lexus, a Division of Toyota Motor Sales, U.S.A., Inc.

Driver's Seat. Published by Toyota Motor Sales, U.S.A., Inc.

Stories and quotes by Kevin Hunter in Chapters 6 and 10 are drawn from author's interview, October 26, 2005.

Quote by Chief Engineer Masao Inoue (Chapter 8) appears courtesy of Toyota Motor Corporation and Kevin Roberts, CEO Worldwide, Saatchi & Saatchi, author of *Lovemarks: The Future Beyond Brands.* Saatchi & Saatchi. Powerhouse Books, New York, New York. 2004. Reprinted with permission.

Images in Chapter 7 appear courtesy of TMS North American Parts Operation, and University of Toyota. Learning Map® is a registered trademark of Root Learning Inc., Maumee, Ohio.

Other sources include:

Matthew E. May, "Eight Simple Lessons from Toyota on Continuous Innovation," *Six Sigma Lean (6L),* April/May 2005.

———— "Innovative Armstrong Changes the Way We Compete," *USA Today,* July 21, 2005.

———— "Lean Thinking for Knowledge Work," *Quality Progress,* June 2005.

———— "The Perils of Bias," *Consulting to Management,* Volume 16, No. 13, September 2005.

Thornton Oxnard, "Stretch! How Toyota Reaches for Big Goals," *Supply Chain Management Review,* March 2004.

The non-Toyota stories, sidebars, quotes, and images in the book were compiled from personal knowledge or from sources readily available to the public, including newspapers (e.g., *The New York Times, The Los Angeles Times, The Wall Street Journal*), magazines (e.g., *Time, Newsweek, Business-Week, Fast Company*), television (e.g., CNN, CNBC, *CBS Sunday Morning*), press releases, newswires, radio, speeches, lectures, and Internet Web sites.

Acknowledgments

Obviously without the rather incredible Toyota organization and my engagements with various parts of it, there would be nothing to write about, and no book. Warm thanks goes to a few special individuals who helped me in some form or fashion, whether they knew it or not, and from whom I've learned more than my fair share: Karin Accomando, Jane Beseda, Will Decker, Matt Gonzales, Dave Harbuck, Kevin Hunter, Ron Johnson, Joe Kane, Toshi Kitamura, Charlotte Lassos, Ray Lindland, Kumi Lopez, Mike Morrison, Thor Oxnard, Ken Pilone, Ken Takagi, Midge Waters, and Mike Wells.

Thank you to my book team—that everything worked so smoothly and enjoyably is a testament to your professionalism and artistry: John Willig, my agent at Literary Services Inc., Fred Hills and Bruce Nichols, my editors at Simon & Schuster/Free Press; and Kathryn Hall, publicist, who helped me get this whole thing rolling downhill.

Thank you to the Los Angeles Police Department for inadvertently giving me one of the more powerful lessons in discovering elegant solutions. Special thanks to Deputy Chief Mike Berkow, Capt. Patrick Findley, Commander Eric Lillo, Lt. Dave Mcgill, Lt. Robert Hauck, Lt. Ricardo DeMartinez, and Lt. James West.

Thanks also to Kerry Morrison of the Hollywood Business Improvement District for allowing me to tell your story. Likewise, to the executive team at Quadrant Homes.

Thanks go as well to my "advisory board" of early readers, for your feedback truly strengthened the book.

And at home, thanks to the four special ladies in my life—Deva, Morgan, Kendal, and Koreen—for making sure I never go out of style, and for being so patient during the six months or so in which I disappeared with a glass of wine every night from nine to one to tap out this little tome.

This was fun.

Index

About the Author

Matthew May partners as an advisor with corporate leaders to help guide change and drive innovation in their organizations. He is the director of Aevitas, a Los Angeles-based firm that works with teams to instill a strong discipline around constant innovation, using a unique blend of logic and creativity to embed the routines they need to build a balanced portfolio of ideas from the front line to the boardroom.

For over eight years Matthew partnered with the University of Toyota, headquartered in Torrance, California, playing a key role in the organizational learning strategy, designing and delivering core programs for Toyota associates both domestically and internationally, as well as instructing and consulting with companies and organizations enrolled in external Toyota programs and workshops focused on achieving excellence in operational innovation, including Wells Fargo, Nextel, Quadrant Homes, Department of Defense, Gallup, Saatchi & Saatchi, Los Angeles Police Department, and various Toyota affiliates.

In addition to Toyota, Matt's clientele in the past has included a number of well-known companies, including Dial Corporation, JD Power and Associates, Nissan, Harley-Davidson, Hyundai, Infiniti, Sandy Corporation, Maritz Performance Improvement, and Sierra Pacific Constructors.

A graduate of The Wharton School and of The Johns Hopkins University, Matthew's expertise is in systems thinking, corporate creativity, complex problem solving, and fast-cycle learning.

He lives with his small family in Westlake Village, California, where he is an avid cyclist.

www.aevitas.com
www.elegantsolutionbook.com